# COLORADO'S
## Lost Creek Wilderness

**CLASSIC SUMMIT HIKES**

# COLORADO'S
## Lost Creek Wilderness

**CLASSIC SUMMIT HIKES**

Gerry Roach & Jennifer Roach

FULCRUM PUBLISHING
Golden, Colorado

Hiking is an inherently dangerous activity and depends on both the good decision-making and safe hiking technique of the hiker. The information contained in this book is based upon the experiences of the authors and might not be perceived as accurate by other persons. This book is not a substitute for sound judgment. Extreme care should be taken when following any of the routes or techniques described in this book. This book is intended for use by hikers and climbers who have the requisite training, experience and knowledge. It is not intended to be used as an instructional guide. Proper clothing and equipment are essential when attempting to hike any of the routes described in this book. Failure to have the requisite experience, equipment and conditioning may subject you to extreme physical danger, including injury and death. The safety of the routes described in this book, as well as any associated dangers, may have changed since the book's publication. Maps pictured in this book are for route definition only; use updated, full-scale USGS quadrangles for actual hikes. Neither Fulcrum Publishing nor the authors assume any liability for injury, damage to property or violation of the law that may arise from the use of this book.

There are no warranties, either express or implied, that the information contained within this book is reliable. There are no warranties that extend beyond the description on the face hereof. Use of this book indicates the user's assumption of risk that it may contain errors, as well as acknowledgment that the user is solely accountable for his or her own abilities to hike in a safe and responsible manner.

Library of Congress Cataloging-in-Publication Data

Roach, Gerry.
  Lost Creek Wilderness : classic summit hikes / Gerry Roach and
Jennifer Roach.
      p. cm.
Includes index.
  ISBN 1-55591-238-9
  1. Hiking—Colorado—Lost Creek Wilderness—Guidebooks. 2. Lost Creek
Wilderness (Colo.)—Guidebooks. I. Roach, Jennifer. II. Title.
  GV199.42.C62 L677 2001
  917.88'59—dc21
                                  00-013216

Printed in Canada
0  9  8  7  6  5  4  3  2  1

Editorial: Daniel Forrest-Bank, Sherri Schultz
Design: Alice C. Merrill
Cartography: Gerry Roach
Front cover photographs: Background—heavy snowmelt dams up Lost Creek, forming a temporary lake. Copyright © 2000 Eric Wunrow. Inset—Digital Imagery Copyright © 2001 PhotoDisc, Inc.
Back cover photograph: A Tarryall afternoon. Copyright © Gerry Roach.
Frontispiece: A rock pinnacle on Bison Arm dwarfs hiker Mike Butyn. Copyright © Gerry Roach.
Interior drawings: Jon MacManus

Fulcrum Publishing
16100 Table Mountain Parkway, Suite 300 • Golden, Colorado 80403
(800) 992-2908 • (303) 277-1623
www.fulcrum-books.com

*This book is dedicated to the animals
that call the wilderness home.*

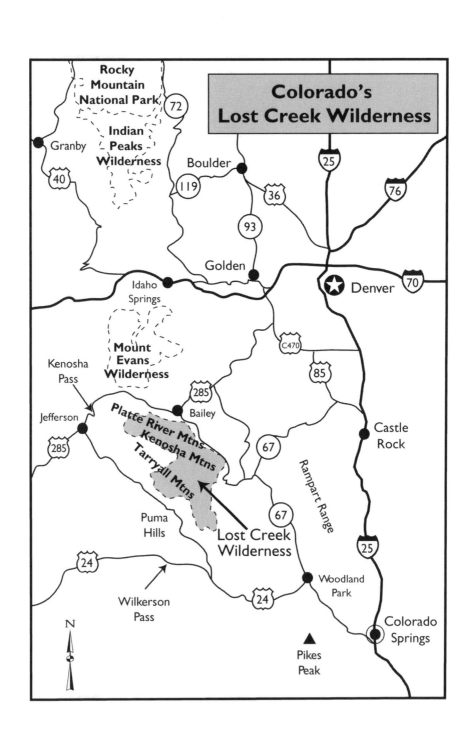

Colorado's Lost Creek Wilderness

# CONTENTS

*A vision without a task is but a dream,*
*A task without a vision is drudgery,*
*A vision and a task is the hope of the world.*

—from a church in Sussex, England

# PREFACE

*by Jennifer Roach*

Colorado's Lost Creek Wilderness is only 40 miles from Denver, and it can richly satisfy your desire for solitude. Every season is a delight, and you can roam freely here throughout the year.

Winter's cold, snowy months are an especially wonderful season to behold. The Lost Creek Wilderness is a place of beauty and mystery where pale winter light mixes the primary colors of granite, evergreens and windswept tundra as an artist mixes paints on a palette. This special place is gentle to the mind and soul. Winter's icy blasts and harsh environment do not often penetrate this place. Welcome to the Lost Creek Wilderness.

This beautiful area has drawn me since my first Colorado mountain out-ings. My first trips explored Payne Gulch and the Craig Creek drainage. Later excursions enabled me to climb some of the famous peaks of the Lost Creek Wilderness. It has always amazed me that I could bushwhack through dense trees, then abruptly emerge onto incredible alpine summit plateaus. On peaks like Windy, Peak X, Lost Platte and Shawnee, you can have such an experience. Then I climbed the monarchs of the Tarryall Range: Bison and McCurdy. These peaks lie atop windswept, open terrain. Views and magic were everywhere, and I was hooked.

Photo opportunities here have always been endless for me. My favorite photos include Bison's great rock monolith and Lost Creek's hidden canyon, where the creek disappears. I have visited the beauties of this wilderness area on every calendar page and always find it a pleasing place to be. I discovered that when deep snow lies on the north slopes, the south slopes often remain sunny and inviting. Avalanche danger here is largely nonexistent. When warm Chinook winds melt the snow from the rocks, a hike up Eagle Rock or one of the Twin Cone Peaks is my cure for cabin fever.

Those frustrated with traffic on Interstate 70 will soon discover that hikes into this Pike National Forest paradise avoid the often-pokey com-mute. The little mountain ranges of the Lost Creek Wilderness provide varied and interesting hiking opportunities. Your outings can vary from short jaunts to epic sojourns. Since much of your time is spent below treeline, you can do many of these summit hikes in less than perfect weather conditions.

The Lost Creek Wilderness is more protected than its higher mountain neighbors to the west.

As spring makes its slow return to Colorado's high country, the Lost Creek Wilderness often has a quicker thaw. Trails open a month earlier, affording hiking and backpacking opportunities for those with spring fever. In April and May, I have hiked with my snowshoes on, yet have been comfortable in shirtsleeves while watching a spring storm lash out at the high country 20 miles away. Flowers appear early; tiny creeks bubble merrily into the Tarryall and Lost Creek drainages as plants turn green and spring warmth reigns.

Summer and fall offer limitless backpacking opportunities on an extensive trail network. The secret places are now open for exploration. It was in fall that I discovered a natural arch near Goose Creek. I also visited and marveled at the secluded Box Canyon along Lost Creek. When fall wanes and the first snows touch the high country, the Lost Creek Wilderness remains snow free. Winter's snows have always been less painful to me knowing that I could happily venture up South Tarryall Peak or Farnum Peak with success.

Every journey into this lovely wilderness has brought me an incredible feeling of isolation and peace. I find it in the scenery and the solitude. This paradise lies close to Denver, yet I rarely encounter other hikers. There is a sense of wonderment in the Lost Creek Wilderness that draws me back for multiple excursions. I hope your opportunities to experience this grand place are limitless.

# INTRODUCTION

*Colorado's Lost Creek Wilderness: Classic Summit Hikes* is a celebration of the hiking joys in and around the Lost Creek Wilderness. Have you ever scooted over Kenosha Pass headed for a fourteener and sped past the Lost Park Road? If you thought about the mountains to the east at all, perhaps you wondered, "What's over there? Lost Park sounds interesting, but I'll check it out when I'm retired." Don't wait too long. What's over there is the Lost Creek Wilderness with its myriad box canyons, crooked creeks, twisty trails, rock towers, arches and 150 peaks, most of them ranked. Let the fourteeners rest for a weekend and check it out.

Congress designated the 120,151-acre Lost Creek Wilderness in 1980, with additions in 1993, as an area offering "outstanding opportunities for solitude or a primitive and unconfined type of recreation." The center of the Lost Creek Wilderness is only 40 miles southwest of downtown Denver. That fact makes this area extremely valuable as a place of peace where you can retreat from the city. You can do most of the hikes in this book in one day from Front Range cities. The hikes all lead to the summit of a peak. The highest summits in the Lost Creek Wilderness rise only a few hundred feet above treeline, but the summit plateaus are special places. You can hike for hours through trees, then burst upon a private universe far above roads and cities. These summits let you taste freedom and touch the sky. They will draw you back.

The highways surrounding the Lost Creek Wilderness are Park County 67 to the east, U.S. 285 to the north and west, and U.S. 24 to the south. The wilderness covers much of three small ranges: the Platte River Mountains, the Kenosha Mountains and the Tarryall Mountains. A fourth area, the nearby Puma Hills, is included in this book for completeness. We refer to these four ranges as the Retirement Range. The Lost Creek Wilderness and most of the area around it is in the Pike National Forest.

Our trailheads are places that passenger cars can reach. Four-wheel-drive vehicles can shorten many Colorado ascents, but one thing is certain: You cannot drive into the Lost Creek Wilderness. Never lose your spirit of discovery. Hike into the wilderness!

## Safety First

Climbing is dangerous and each individual should approach these peaks with caution. Conditions can vary tremendously depending on time of day and time of year. The route descriptions in this book assume good, summer conditions. Lightning is always a serious hazard in Colorado during the summer months. Snow conditions vary from year to year.

Before charging forth with your city energy and competitive urges, take some time to understand the mountain environment you are about to enter. Carefully study your chosen route and do not be afraid to retreat if your condition, or the mountain's, is unfavorable. Better yet, do an easier hike nearby to become familiar with the area. When both you and the mountain are ready, come back and do your dream hike.

### Lightning

Colorado is famous for apocalyptic lightning storms that threaten not just your life, but your soul as well. This section will have special meaning if you have ever been trapped by a storm that endures for more than an hour and leaves no gap between one peal of thunder and the next. The term *simultaneous flash-boom* has a very personal meaning for many Colorado hikers.

*Dangers*
- Lightning is the greatest external hazard to summer mountaineering in Colorado.
- Lightning kills people every year in Colorado's mountains.
- Direct hits are usually fatal.

*Precautions*
- Start early! Be off summits by noon and back in the valley by early afternoon.
- Observe thunderhead buildup carefully, noting speed and direction; towering thunderheads with black bottoms are bad.
- When lightning begins nearby, count the seconds between flash and thunder, then divide by 5 to calculate the distance to the flash in miles. Repeat to determine if lightning is approaching.
- Try to determine if the lightning activity is cloud-to-cloud or ground strikes.
- Get off summits and ridges.

*Protection*
- You cannot outrun a storm; physics wins.
- When caught, seek a safe zone in the 45-degree cone around an object 5 to 10 times your height.

- Be aware of ground currents; the current from a ground strike disperses along the ground or cliff, especially in wet cracks.
- Wet items are good conductors; snow is not a good conductor.
- Separate yourself from metal objects.
- Avoid sheltering in spark gaps under boulders and trees.
- Disperse the group. Survivors can revive one who is hit.
- Crouch on boot soles, ideally on dry, insulating material such as moss or grass. Dirt is better than rock. Avoid water.
- Do not put your hands down. Put elbows on knees and hands on head. This gives current a short path through your arms rather than the longer path through your vital organs.
- Do not lie down; current easily goes through your vital organs.

### First Aid
- Know and give CPR. Many lightning-strike victims have been revived by CPR.
- Treat for burns; evacuate.

## Leave No Trace

If you use the wilderness resource, it is your responsibility to help protect it from environmental damage. The old adage "Take nothing but pictures; leave nothing but footprints" is no longer good enough. Visitors' footprints can cause extensive damage to fragile alpine areas. The ground plants above treeline are especially vulnerable because they cling to a tenuous existence. If you destroy a patch of tundra with a careless step, it may take a hundred years for the plants to recover. In some cases, they may never recover.

Most of the routes in this book reach the alpine zone. Tread lightly. Stay on the trails, and where trails do not exist, travel on durable surfaces like rock and snow. Walk on rocks in the tundra, not on the tundra itself. If traveling over tundra is the only option, be sure to disperse use over a wide area. Let your eyes do the walking sometimes. You do not have to explore every inch on foot. Respect the environment you are entering. If you do not show respect, you are an intruder, not a visitor.

Leave No Trace (LNT), a national nonprofit organization dedicated to educating people about responsible use of the outdoors, recommends a few simple techniques for minimum-impact travel through fragile alpine environments. Learn them. Abide by them. For more information about LNT and minimum-impact outdoor ethics, visit the LNT website at www.lnt.org or call (800) 332-4100. The six tenets of the LNT movement are:

### 1. Plan Ahead and Prepare
- Know the regulations and special concerns of the area you are visiting.
- Visit the backcountry in small groups.

- Avoid popular areas during times of high use.
- Choose equipment and clothing in subdued colors.
- Repackage food into reusable containers.

## 2. Camp and Travel on Durable Surfaces
### On the Trail
- Stay on designated trails. Walk in single file in the middle of the path.
- Do not shortcut switchbacks; this can cause severe erosion.
- Where multiple trails exist, choose the one that is most worn.
- Where no trails exist, spread out across the terrain.
- When traveling cross-country, choose the most durable surfaces available: rock, gravel, dry grasses or snow.
- Rest on rock or in designated sites.
- Avoid wetlands and riparian areas.
- Use a map and compass to eliminate the need for rock cairns, tree scars and ribbons.
- Step to the downhill side of the trail and talk softly when encountering pack stock.

### At Camp
- Choose an established, legal site that will not be damaged by your stay.
- Camping above treeline is not recommended because of damage to tundra plants.
- Restrict activities to the area where vegetation is compacted or absent.
- Keep pollutants out of water sources by camping at least 200 feet (70 adult steps) from lakes and streams.
- Move campsites frequently.

## 3. Pack It In, Pack It Out
- Pack everything that you bring into wild country back out with you.
- Protect wildlife and your food by storing rations securely.
- Pick up all spilled foods.

## 4. Properly Dispose of What You Can't Pack Out
- Deposit human waste in catholes dug 6 to 8 inches deep at least 200 feet from water, camp or trails. Cover and disguise the cathole when finished.
- Use toilet paper or wipes sparingly. Pack them out.
- To wash yourself or your dishes, carry water 200 feet away from streams or lakes, and use small amounts of biodegradable soap. Strain and scatter dish water; pack out remaining particles.
- Inspect your campsite for trash and evidence of your stay. Pack out all trash: yours and others.

### 5. Leave What You Find

- Treat our national heritage with respect. Leave plants, rocks and historical artifacts as you find them for others to discover and enjoy.
- Good campsites are found, not made. Altering a site should not be necessary.
- Observe wildlife quietly from a distance; never feed wild animals.
- Let nature's sounds prevail. Keep loud voices and noises to a minimum.
- Control pets at all times. Remove dog feces.
- Do not build structures or furniture, or dig trenches.

### 6. Minimize Use and Impact of Fires

- Campfires can cause lasting impacts to the backcountry. Always carry a lightweight stove for cooking. Enjoy a candle lantern instead of a fire.
- When fires are permitted, use established fire rings, fire pans or mound fires. Do not scar large rocks or overhangs.
- Gather sticks no larger than an adult's wrist.
- Do not snap branches off live, dead or downed trees.
- Put out campfires completely.
- Remove all unburned trash from fire ring and scatter the cool ashes over a large area far from camp.

*Beautiful but tenuous life near the Brookside-McCurdy Trail*

## The Rating System

We have used a simple system to rate each hike. Each hike's rating has four numbers: R Points, round-trip mileage, round-trip elevation gain and Class.

We present these four numbers right below the route name.

The R Point number is a measure of the *effort* the hike requires. It summarizes distance, elevation gain and difficulty into one number. You can compare the R Point numbers for two hikes and know which one requires more effort. You can also use the R Point number to determine how long the hike will take. Hiking speeds vary, but most hikers average 20 to 25 R Points per hour. For example, if you have determined that you can average 25 R Points per hour, and a route has a rating of 150 R Points, then your projected time for that hike is 6 hours.

The round-trip mileage is just that. The round-trip elevation gain includes any extra gain you may encounter going over passes or false summits both on the ascent and on the return.

The Class indicates the hiking difficulty. The hikes in this book are either Class 1 or Class 2. Class 1 is trail hiking or any hiking across open country that is no more difficult than walking on a maintained trail. The parking lot at the trailhead is easy Class 1, groomed trails are mid-range Class 1 and big step-ups are difficult Class 1. Class 2 is off-trail hiking, usually bushwhacking or hiking on a talus slope. You are not yet using handholds for upward movement. Occasionally, we use the rating Class 2+ for a route where you will use your hands, but do not need to search very hard for handholds. We call this scampering.

*Winter solitude on Bison Arm*

**Here is a sampling of the R Point numbers for several Front Range hikes:**

  26   Mount Sanitas via Dakota Ridge
  44   Green Mountain via Saddle Rock
  67   South Boulder Peak via Shadow Canyon
  83   "Puma Peak" North Slopes
101   "Peak X" Southeast Slopes
120   Mount Audubon Trail
148   Grays Peak Trail
157   Bison Peak Southwest Ridge
187   McCurdy Mountain South Slopes
376   Longs Peak Keyhole Route
418   Pikes Peak via Barr Trail

**You might choose to rely on the standard 10 essentials:**

1. Map
2. Compass
3. Sunglasses and sunscreen
4. Extra food
5. Extra clothing
6. Headlamp/flashlight
7. First-aid supplies
8. Fire starter
9. Matches
10. Knife

**Gerry relies on his Classic Commandments of Mountaineering:**

Never get separated from your lunch.
Never get separated from your sleeping bag.
Never get separated from your primal urges.
Carefully consider where your primal urges are leading you.
Expect to go the wrong way some of the time.
First aid above 26,000 feet consists of getting below 26,000 feet.
Never step on the rope.
Never bivouac.
Surfer Girl is not in the mountains.
Never pass up a chance to pee.
Don't eat yellow snow.
Experience does not exempt you from danger; physics wins.
Have fun and remember why you started.

*Vaya con Dios!*

*And this our life,*
*exempt from public haunt,*
*Finds tongues in trees, books in the*
*running brooks,*
*Sermons in stones, and good in everything.*
*I would not change it.*

—William Shakespeare

# chapter one

# Platte River Mountains

## Introduction

Our journey starts here. Many hikers drive on U.S. 285 zooming to distant adventures. You may have scanned the long skyline ridge to the southwest as you approached Bailey. You may have noticed the dirt road heading east from the top of Kenosha Pass and wondered where it went. These are the Platte River Mountains. Once you have sampled one of these summits, you are likely to return for more. The hikes are arduous, but the open summits let you touch the sky.

In this chapter, we describe every named or ranked peak over 10,200 feet in the Platte River Mountains. All these summits are in the Pike National Forest, and all but one are in the Lost Creek Wilderness. We describe the summits from northwest to southeast.

The boundary of the Platte River Mountains is rather confusing for such a small range. Simply stated, the range is the ridge of mountains south of U.S. 285 between Bailey and Kenosha Pass. A more detailed description follows.

The boundary of the Platte River Mountains is the North Fork of the South Platte River on the north and Craig Creek on the east and south to the 11,540-foot saddle 0.7 mile west of Point 11,941. The boundary is then a straight line between this saddle and the 11,660-foot saddle 0.6 mile south of Foster Benchmark. Rock Creek is the range boundary south from this saddle to Tarryall Creek. Tarryall Creek is the range boundary on the southwest. Finally, U.S. 285 is the range boundary between Tarryall Creek and Webster on the North Fork of the South Platte River. A list of all the summits in the Platte River Mountains is in the Appendix.

See
map I,
page 3

# 1. TWIN CONE GROUP

| | |
|---|---|
| **North Twin Cone Peak** | **12,323 feet** |
| **Mount Blaine** | **12,303 feet** |
| **South Twin Cone Peak** | **12,340 feet** |

These peaks form the anchor for the Retirement Range. They are 3 to 4 miles west of Kenosha Pass on U.S. 285. Because this major highway curves around these peaks, there are three trailheads giving good access to the heights. You can park just off the pavement and be on a summit in a few hours. Each of these peaks has its accolades. Together, they are more than a quarter of all the twelvers in the Retirement Range.

## Maps

*Required: Mount Logan*
*Optional: Jefferson, Observatory Rock*

## Trailheads

### Kenosha Pass Trailhead

This trailhead is at 10,060 feet and provides access to North Twin Cone's west side. Go to 9,980-foot Kenosha Pass on U.S. 285. Kenosha Pass is 8.0 miles west of Bailey and 4.2 miles northeast of Jefferson. Fifty yards south of the sign at the summit of Kenosha Pass, turn east onto FS 126 (dirt) and measure from this point. Go east on FS 126, stay south (right) at 0.2 mile

*Twin Cone Peaks from Observatory Rock*

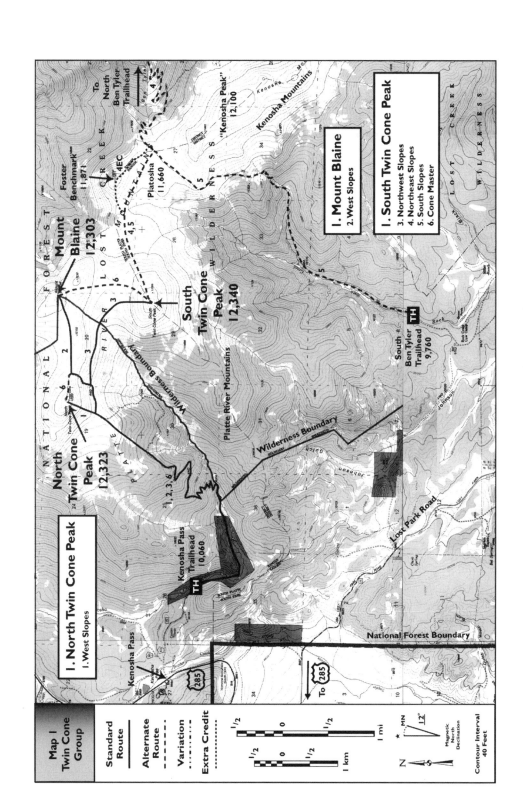

Map 1
Twin Cone Group

I. North Twin Cone Peak
1. West Slopes

Mount Blaine 12,303

North Twin Cone Peak 12,323

South Twin Cone Peak 12,340

"Kenosha Peak" 12,100

Foster Benchmark 11,871

Platosha 11,660

Kenosha Mountains

Kenosha Pass

Platte River Mountains

Wilderness Boundary

National Forest Boundary

Wilderness Boundary

To North Ben Tyler Trailhead

South Ben Tyler Trailhead 9,760

Kenosha Pass Trailhead 10,060

LOST CREEK WILDERNESS

NATIONAL FOREST

Johnson Gulch

Lost Park Road

To 285

285

I. Mount Blaine
2. West Slopes

I. South Twin Cone Peak
3. Northwest Slopes
4. Northeast Slopes
5. South Slopes
6. Cone Master

Standard Route
Alternate Route
Variation
Extra Credit

N
MN
12°
Magnetic North Declination

½   0   ½   1 mi
½   0   ½   1 km

Contour Interval 40 Feet

and continue east then southeast to a gate at 1.0 mile where the road reaches Kenosha Creek. This is the trailhead.

This is one of only three trailheads in this book that are over 10,000 feet. Nevertheless, in summer, four-wheel-drive vehicles may be able to go farther. In winter, you can often get close to this trailhead. You can always park on Kenosha Pass and walk the extra mile.

### North Ben Tyler Trailhead

This trailhead is at 8,260 feet and provides access to South Twin Cone, "Platte Peak" and Shawnee Peak. The trailhead is on U.S. 285 and you can approach it from the east or west. For the eastern approach, go 6.5 miles west on U.S. 285 from the junction of Park County 64 and U.S. 285 in Bailey. For the western approach, go 11.5 miles east on U.S. 285 from the summit of Kenosha Pass. The trailhead is on the south side of the highway. There is a sign for the Ben Tyler Trail and a small parking area here. There is also a narrow parking area across from the trailhead on the north side of the highway. This trailhead is accessible in winter.

### South Ben Tyler Trailhead

This trailhead is at 9,760 feet and provides access to South Twin Cone's south side. If approaching from the east, go 3.0 miles southwest on U.S. 285 from the summit of Kenosha Pass. If approaching from the south, go 1.2 miles northeast on U.S. 285 from the small town of Jefferson. Turn east on Park County 56 (Lost Park Road) and measure from this point.

Go east on Park County 56 and enter the Pike National Forest at 1.9 miles. The road becomes FS 56 at this point. It is still Lost Park Road. Continue southeast on Lost Park Road, stay east (left) at 5.1 miles and turn north (left) onto FS 133 (Rock Creek Road) at 7.0 miles. Go north on Rock Creek Road, pass Rock Creek Trailhead and the Colorado Trail at 8.1 miles and reach South Ben Tyler Trailhead at 9.0 miles. The Lost Creek Wilderness is just north of the trailhead. Winter access is usually from the Lost Park–Rock Creek Road junction.

## 1. North Twin Cone Peak    12,323 feet

See map 1, page 3

North Twin Cone Peak is 3.2 miles east-northeast of Kenosha Pass and U.S. 285. North Twin Cone is the fourth-highest peak in the Retirement Range and is one of nine ranked twelvers in the range. North Twin Cone also has the distinction of being the westernmost peak in this book. It is appropriate to start our journey here. You can see the peak from Kenosha Pass, but you get a better view from South Park near Jefferson. North Twin Cone is a gentle peak. It is not in the Lost Creek Wilderness, and there is a four-wheel-drive road to the summit and a building on top. In spite of this, the peak provides a worthwhile outing to a high, open summit.

**Route**
### 1.1 West Slopes
*From Kenosha Pass TH at 10,060 ft:     107 RP     9.0 mi     2,263 ft     Class 1*

This is the easiest route on North Twin Cone Peak. You can use the summit road for much of your ascent. Start at Kenosha Pass Trailhead and hike 0.4 mile south on the road along Kenosha Creek's west side. Cross to the creek's east side and hike 0.1 mile south up the drainage to a sharp turn to the east. Hike 1.0 mile east-northeast on the road along Kenosha Creek's north side to 10,370 feet. The introduction is over as the road begins a steep ascent here.

Follow the road 2.0 miles north then northeast through many switchbacks to 11,300 feet. The main road descends to the east from here. Leave the main road and hike 0.5 mile northeast on a faint road to treeline at 11,600 feet. You can finally see the summit from here. Rejoin the main road and hike 0.2 mile north on it to 11,780 feet below the summit. When the road contours east, leave it and hike 0.3 mile north-northeast on tundra to the summit. You can also follow the road from 11,780 feet to the summit. This route is 0.7 mile longer than the direct finish.

5

# 1. Mount Blaine     12,303 feet

See map 1, page 3

Mount Blaine is 1.2 miles west of North Twin Cone Peak. Mount Blaine is a shy peak. Blaine is only 2.2 miles north of U.S. 285, but few motorists notice it. When you try to see Blaine from South Park, it hides behind North and South Twin Cones. Perhaps Blaine is shy because it is unranked. Nevertheless, Blaine has three distinctions. Unlike North Twin Cone, Mount Blaine is on the edge of the Lost Creek Wilderness. Mount Blaine is the northernmost peak in this book. Better, Mount Blaine is the only summit in the Retirement Range that has the appellation "Mount." Normally, the word Mount is reserved for the highest, grandest summits—like Mount Everest. Thus, Mount Blaine touches greatness.

**Route**
### 1.2 West Slopes
*From Kenosha Pass TH at 10,060 ft:     125 RP     11.4 mi     2,243 ft     Class 1*

This is the shortest route on mighty Mount Blaine. Start at Kenosha Pass Trailhead and follow North Twin Cone's West Slopes Route to 11,780 feet. Stay on the road and follow it 0.6 mile as it contours east then ascends north to 12,100 feet in the west end of the long, flat saddle between North Twin

Cone and Blaine. Leave the road and hike 0.9 mile east to Blaine's boulder-strewn summit.

See map 1, page 3

# 1. South Twin Cone Peak    12,340 feet

South Twin Cone Peak is 1.4 miles southeast of North Twin Cone Peak and 1.1 miles south of Mount Blaine. South Twin Cone may not be a Mount, but it is in the Lost Creek Wilderness; it's also the third-highest peak in the Retirement Range and the highest peak in the Platte River Mountains. It also offers a choice of routes. After your hike, you can gaze at South Twin Cone from South Park and impress friends with your knowledge of the horizon.

6

*South Twin Cone Peak from the southeast*

## Routes

### 1.3 Northwest Slopes

*From Kenosha Pass TH at 10,060 ft:    157 RP    11.6 mi    2,280 ft    Class 2*

This is the shortest route on South Twin Cone Peak. It is rougher than the hikes up North Twin Cone and Blaine. Start at Kenosha Pass Trailhead and follow North Twin Cone's West Slopes Route to treeline at 11,600 feet. From here, you can see South Twin Cone 1.3 miles southeast. Avoid any temptation to head straight for the peak, as there is an ocean of bushes between it and you. You need to hike above the bushes. Hike 0.2 mile north on the road to 11,780 feet. Contour 0.3 mile east on the road. When the road ascends north, leave it and contour 0.9 mile east then southeast to a point at 11,800 feet directly north of South Twin Cone's summit. There are many bushes in this area, and it is difficult to avoid them all. Hike 0.4 mile south up a rough slope to the summit and a commanding view.

### 1.4 Northeast Slopes
*From North Ben Tyler TH at 8,260 ft: 220 RP   14.4 mi   4,280 ft   Class 2*

This is a longer but easier route on South Twin Cone Peak. Most of the hike is on a good trail. It is also a shorter drive if you are coming from Denver. You can spend your time hiking instead of driving. Start at North Ben Tyler Trailhead and hike 4.3 miles southwest up the Ben Tyler Trail to a trail junction at 11,000 feet. Turn west (right) and hike 1.3 miles west into the broad 11,660-foot saddle between South Twin Cone and "Kenosha Peak." From here, you can see South Twin Cone 1.5 miles west of the saddle.

This saddle is the northwest end of the Kenosha Mountains and is the point where the Kenosha Mountains and the Platte River Mountains meet. This lofty meeting place is called Platosha. Leave the trail in Platosha and hike 0.5 mile northwest, descending slightly en route to 11,560 feet at the head of a shallow basin. Dodging bushes, hike 1.1 miles west to the summit.

### 1.4EC Extra Credit—Foster Benchmark    11,871 feet

Foster Benchmark is 1.4 miles east-northeast of South Twin Cone. From Platosha, hike 0.5 mile north-northwest to Foster Benchmark's unique summit (Class 2).

### 1.5 South Slopes *Classic*
*From South Ben Tyler TH at 9,760 ft: 171 RP   11.2 mi   2,780 ft   Class 2*

This is an interesting, easy route on South Twin Cone Peak. If you are approaching from Denver, your drive to the trailhead is longer but, depending on the season, the south-facing approach hike may be an equitable trade. Start at South Ben Tyler Trailhead and hike 4.0 miles north-northwest up Rock Creek on the Ben Tyler Trail to Platosha, the 11,660-foot saddle between South Twin Cone Peak and "Kenosha Peak." Join the Northeast Slopes Route here and follow it to the summit.

# 1. Twin Cones and Blaine Combination
### 1.6 Cone Master *Classic*
*From Kenosha Pass TH at 10,060 ft:    170 RP   12.6 mi   2,866 ft   Class 2*

See map 1, page 3

This is the easiest way to ascend both Twin Cones and Mount Blaine together. This easy hike is only slightly longer than any one of the peaks, and it is a nice way to ascend the third-, fourth- and fifth-highest peaks in the Retirement Range. Start at Kenosha Pass Trailhead and ascend North Twin Cone's West Slopes Route. From North Twin Cone's summit, descend 0.3 mile east on the road to the west edge of the flat, 12,100-foot saddle between

7

8

*South Twin Cone from the west*

North Twin Cone and Blaine. Hike 0.5 mile east across this long saddle, then hike 0.4 mile east-northeast to Blaine's summit. Descend 0.6 mile south-southeast to the 11,940-foot Blaine-South Twin Cone saddle. There are many bushes in this broad saddle. Hike 0.5 mile south then west to South Twin Cone's summit. Descend South Twin Cone's Northwest Slopes Route.

See map 2, page 9

## 2. PLATTE PEAK GROUP

| "Platte Peak" | 11,941 feet |
| Shawnee Peak | 11,927 feet |

These two peaks are on the main ridge of the Platte River Mountains above U.S. 285. They are halfway between Bailey and Kenosha Pass. Shawnee is the most visible peak on this ridge, and there is a small town called Shawnee on

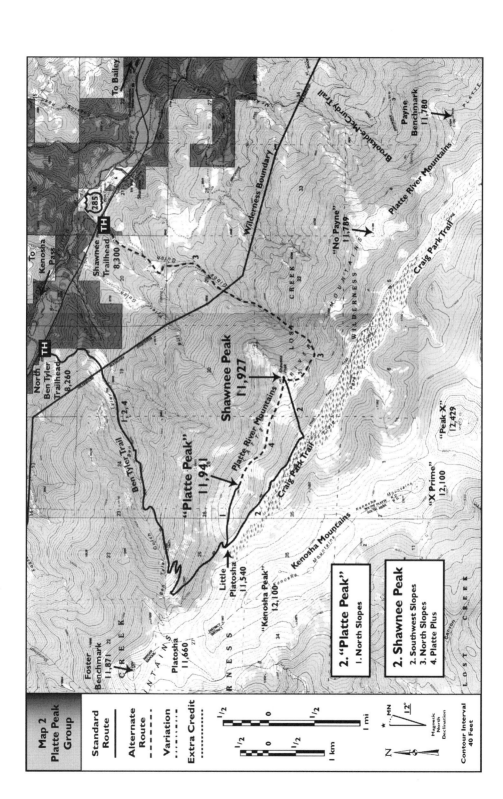

U.S. 285. These are classic Retirement Range summits. The massif is mostly tree covered, but the summits are rocky and open with expansive views. Both peaks are in the Lost Creek Wilderness.

## Maps
*Required: Shawnee*

## Trailhead
### Shawnee Trailhead
This trailhead is at 8,300 feet and provides access to Shawnee's north side. If approaching from the east, go 5.0 miles east on U.S. 285 from the junction of Park County 64 and U.S. 285 in Bailey. If approaching from the west, go 13.0 miles east on U.S. 285 from the summit of Kenosha Pass. Turn south onto FS 115, go 100 yards south, go through a gate in a fence and park. This is the trailhead. This is Forest Service land and there is a Forest Service sign here. The access gate is locked and four-wheel-drive vehicles cannot go farther. This trailhead is accessible in winter.

See map 2, page 9

# 2. "Platte Peak"    11,941 feet

"Platte Peak" is 3.5 miles east of South Twin Cone Peak. This summit is seldom visited, perhaps because it is not a twelver and not officially named. After all the excitement of the Twin Cone Group, the range takes a fresh breath here. "Platte Peak" is a ranked and important summit. It is higher than Shawnee. That is sufficient reason to ascend "Platte Peak." The rocky, open summit waits for you.

## Route
### 2.1 North Slopes *Classic*
*From North Ben Tyler TH at 8,260 ft: 140 RP    11.6 mi    3,681 ft    Class 1*

This is the easiest route up "Platte Peak." It is a hike up a good trail with a short stroll to a wonderful summit. Start at North Ben Tyler Trailhead (see Twin Cone Group) and hike 4.3 miles southwest up the Ben Tyler Trail to a trail junction at 11,000 feet. Turn east (left), leave the Ben Tyler Trail and hike 0.8 mile southeast on the Craig Park Trail to the 11,540-foot saddle between "Platte Peak" and "Kenosha Peak." This saddle is called Little Platosha. Leave the trail in Little Platosha and hike 0.2 mile east up a rounded ridge to treeline at 11,760 feet. This is the magic moment where the wooded world falls away and only the summits remain. Hike 0.5 mile east past small rock outcrops to the highest point, which is the farthest outcrop.

From the summit, you can look southeast into Craig Park. Craig Creek separates the Platte River Mountains and the Kenosha Mountains. You can-

**"Platte Peak"**
**11,941**

*"Platte Peak" from "Kenosha Peak"*

not see this drainage from U.S. 285. Little Platosha is where the Platte River Mountains and Kenosha Mountains reluctantly tear themselves apart. Sitting on the summit of "Platte Peak," you can begin to understand the complicated terrain in the Retirement Range.

## 2. Shawnee Peak    11,927 feet

*See map 2, page 9*

Shawnee Peak is 6.5 miles west of Bailey, and you can see the peak's rough, pointed summit from U.S. 285. Shawnee is the showcase peak of the Platte River Mountains. Many look at it, but few ascend it. Shawnee's summit is well guarded by steep, wooded slopes and requires a significant effort to reach. Your effort will be rewarded.

### Routes
#### 2.2 Southwest Slopes
*From North Ben Tyler TH at 8,260 ft: 173 RP    14.6 mi    4,507 ft    Class 1*

This is the easiest route up Shawnee Peak, but it is a long hike. Start at North Ben Tyler Trailhead (see Twin Cone Group) and follow the North Slopes Route on "Platte Peak" to Little Platosha at 11,540 feet. From here, hike 1.5 miles southeast on the Craig Park Trail under the south side of "Platte Peak" to 11,120 feet in Craig Park. Leave the trail here and hike 0.7 mile northeast to Shawnee's summit. You can look south at the six twelvers in the Kenosha Mountains and know that there is more.

*Shawnee Peak from "Platte Peak"*

### 2.3 North Slopes
*From Shawnee TH at 8,300 ft:*      *164 RP*    *7.8 mi*    *3,627 ft*    *Class 2*

This is a shorter, steeper and rougher route up Shawnee Peak. Start at Shawnee Trailhead and hike 0.1 mile east on the road (FS 115), then continue on the road 0.4 mile to a junction. Go straight (right) and follow the road 1.5 miles south-southeast to its end at 9,120 feet in Gibbs Gulch. Hike 0.5 mile up an old trail in Gibbs Gulch to 9,600 feet. When the trail dies, continue 1.0 mile south-southeast up Gibbs Gulch to the 11,420-foot saddle southeast of Shawnee Peak. This bushwhack is the crux of the hike. From the saddle, it is reward time. Hike 0.4 mile northwest through a rock wonderland to the summit.

## 2. "Platte Peak" and Shawnee Combination

See map 2, page 9

### 2.4 Platte Plus *Classic*
*From North Ben Tyler TH at 8,260 ft: 203 RP*    *14.4 mi*    *4,509 ft*    *Class 2*
*With descent of Shawnee's North Slopes:168 RP*    *11.0 mi*    *4,088 ft*    *Class 2*

This is the easiest way to ascend "Platte Peak" and Shawnee Peak together. Start at North Ben Tyler Trailhead (see Twin Cone Group) and ascend the North Slopes Route on "Platte Peak." From the summit of "Platte Peak," hike 1.3 miles east-southeast on the ridge to Shawnee Peak, skirting Point 11,792 en route (Class 2). Descend Shawnee's Southwest Slopes Route.

With a vehicle shuttle, you can descend Shawnee's North Slopes Route to Shawnee Trailhead. It is 1.5 miles between Shawnee Trailhead and North Ben Tyler Trailhead.

# 3. No Payne Group

| | | See map 3, page 14 |
|---|---|---|
| "No Payne" | 11,789 feet | |
| Payne Benchmark | 11,780 feet | |
| "Lost Platte Peak" | 10,657 feet | |

These peaks form the crest of the Platte River Mountains southwest of Bailey. You can see Payne Benchmark and "No Payne" as you descend south toward Bailey on U.S. 285. Both these peaks have open summits. "Lost Platte Peak" is harder to see and has a tree-covered summit. All three peaks are in the Lost Creek Wilderness. These peaks provide great workouts, especially in winter. They are all accessible from Brookside-Payne Trailhead, which is the closest Retirement Range trailhead to Denver.

13

## Maps

*Required: Shawnee, Topaz Mountain, Windy Peak*
*Optional: Bailey*

## Trailhead

### Brookside-Payne Trailhead

This trailhead is at 8,020 feet and provides access to the south sides of "No Payne," Payne Benchmark and "Lost Platte Peak." Go to Bailey on U.S. 285. On the west edge of town, turn south onto Park County 64 and measure from this point. Go west on Park County 64, stay south (left) at 0.4 mile, cross Payne Gulch at 1.7 miles and reach a sign for Brookside-Payne Trailhead at 2.0 miles. Turn south (left) and reach the large trailhead parking area at 2.1 miles. This trailhead is accessible in winter.

## 3. "No Payne"  11,789 feet

See map 3, page 14

"No Payne" is 5.1 miles southwest of Bailey. This seldom-visited summit has a large open area surrounding it. You can just see the edge of the summit plateau from U.S. 285 as you descend Crow Hill toward Bailey. The joy of walking across the plateau is reserved for those willing to take a hike.

## Route

### 3.1 Northeast Slopes *Classic*

*From Brookside-Payne TH at 8,020 ft: 174 RP   13.0 mi   3,849 ft   Class 2*

This is a stiff hike, but it is mostly on a good trail. The Forest Service rerouted the trails in this area to avoid private property. Start at Brookside-Payne Trailhead and hike 0.5 mile southwest on the Brookside-Payne Trail to a broad ridge. Continue 0.6 mile south on the trail to a trail junction in a small saddle at 8,540 feet. The Brookside-McCurdy Trail goes west from here, and the Payne Gulch Trail goes southeast. Turn west (right) and

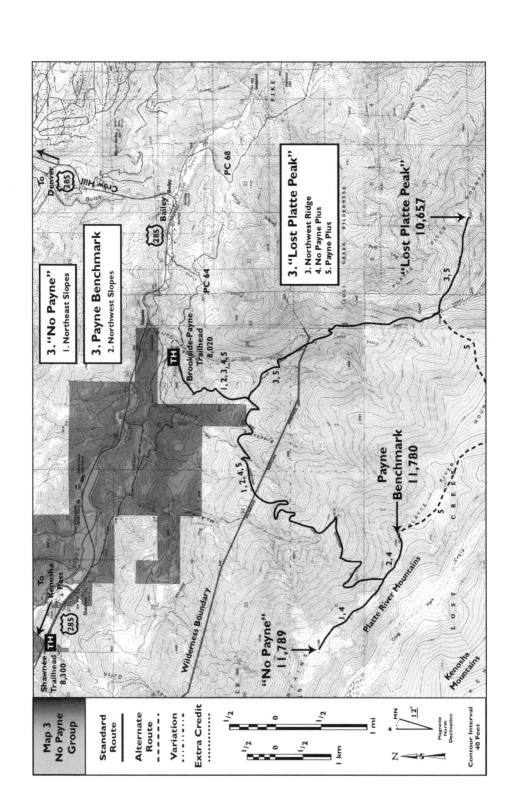

Map 3
No Payne Group

Standard
Route
Alternate
Route
Variation
Extra Credit

Contour Interval
40 Feet

Magnetic
North
Declination

MN 12°

N

1 mi
1 km

3. "No Payne"
1. Northeast Slopes

3. Payne Benchmark
2. Northwest Slopes

3. "Lost Platte Peak"
3. Northwest Ridge
4. No Payne Plus
5. Payne Plus

Shawnee Trailhead
8,300

To Kenosha Pass

To Denver

Crow Hill

Bailey

Brookside-Payne Trailhead
8,020

Wilderness Boundary

"No Payne"
11,789

Payne Benchmark
11,780

"Lost Platte Peak"
10,657

Platte River Mountains

Kenosha Mountains

hike 1.0 mile west then southwest on the rerouted Brookside-McCurdy Trail across both branches of Brookside Creek, and join the original trail at 9,000 feet. The trail is easy to follow from this point.

Hike 0.2 mile southwest on the good trail to the Lost Creek Wilderness boundary. From the wilderness boundary, hike 3.1 miles south on the Brookside-McCurdy Trail to the 11,260-foot saddle between "No Payne" and Payne Benchmark. Your big effort is over. Now you can enjoy the summit ride. Leave the trail and hike 1.1 miles northwest along a broad, remarkable ridge to the summit. The last 0.3 mile is wide open.

15

*Payne Benchmark from the north*

# 3. Payne Benchmark    11,780 feet

See map 3, page 14

Payne Benchmark is 4.3 miles southwest of Bailey and 1.5 miles southeast of "No Payne." Although not as wide open as the summit of "No Payne," Payne Benchmark's secluded, rocky summit is well worth a visit. One of the joys of hikes in the Platte River Mountains is that you start in the city and end up at a viewpoint that allows you to gaze south across many miles of open country.

**Route**

### 3.2 Northwest Slopes *Classic*

*From Brookside-Payne TH at 8,020 ft: 153 RP    11.8 mi    3,760 ft    Class 2*

This is a slightly easier hike than "No Payne." Start at Brookside-Payne Trailhead and follow the Northeast Slopes Route on "No Payne" to the 11,260-foot saddle between "No Payne" and Payne Benchmark. Leave the trail here and hike 0.5 mile east-southeast to the summit. From here, you can continue your study of the Kenosha Mountains.

*Summit of "Lost Platte Peak"*

See map 3, page 14

## 3. "Lost Platte Peak"    10,657 feet

"Lost Platte Peak" is 3.4 miles south of Bailey and 3.4 miles east-southeast of Payne Benchmark. You cannot easily see this hidden summit from highways. In spite of its lower altitude, "Lost Platte Peak" is an isolated, singular summit with a lot of power. It is deeper in the range and requires a healthy hike. This peak's rocky summit provides great views and is for students of the obscure who are game for the gain.

**Route**

### 3.3 Northwest Ridge

*From Brookside-Payne TH at 8,020 ft: 121 RP    10.0 mi    3,083 ft    Class 2*

This hike is wonderful in September when the aspen trees are in full color. Start at Brookside-Payne Trailhead and hike 0.5 mile southwest on the

Brookside-Payne Trail to an old road near a large, fallen tree. Turn east (left) and continue 0.6 mile southeast then south on the trail to a signed trail junction at 8,540 feet, east of a broad saddle. The Brookside-McCurdy Trail goes west from here, and the Payne Gulch Trail goes southeast. Turn east (left) and hike 1.1 miles southeast on the Payne Gulch Trail to the Lost Creek Wilderness boundary at 8,700 feet.

Enter the wilderness, continue 0.2 mile southeast and cross to Payne Creek's east side. The trail to this point is the rerouted Payne Gulch Trail that avoids private property in lower Payne Gulch. Hike 1.4 miles south on the original Payne Gulch Trail to the 9,890-foot saddle between Payne Benchmark and "Lost Platte Peak." You still cannot see the peak you are climbing.

17

Leave the trail in the 9,890-foot saddle and hike 0.2 mile east through an aspen grove to 10,060 feet on the broad, curving northwest ridge of "Lost Platte Peak." Turn south (right) and hike 0.4 mile east-southeast to Point 10,303. It is worth visiting this little summit for the expansive view of Windy Peak to the south. You can also get a peekaboo view of the elusive "Lost Platte Peak" to the east. From Point 10,303, descend 0.1 mile east to 10,180 feet. Now for your summit ride. Hike 0.5 mile east through open aspen glades to the rocky summit. There are three little rock outcrops to choose from. They are all worth a visit for their distinct views. The southernmost outcrop is the highest.

# 3. No Payne Group Combinations

See map 3, page 14

### 3.4 No Payne Plus

*From Brookside-Payne TH at 8,020 ft: 203 RP   14.0 mi   4,369 ft   Class 2*

This is the easiest way to ascend "No Payne" and Payne Benchmark together. Start at Brookside-Payne Trailhead and ascend the Northeast Slopes Route on "No Payne." Return to the 11,260-foot saddle between "No Payne" and Payne Benchmark. Hike 0.5 mile east-southeast to Payne Benchmark's summit. Descend Payne Benchmark's Northwest Slopes Route.

### 3.5 Payne Plus

*From Brookside-Payne TH at 8,020 ft: 289 RP   17.4 mi   5,216 ft   Class 2*

This is the easiest way to ascend "No Payne," Payne Benchmark and "Lost Platte Peak" together. Follow No Payne Plus (Route 3.4) to Payne Benchmark's summit. The fun has just begun. Hike 3.2 miles southeast then northeast to the 9,890-foot saddle between Payne Benchmark and "Lost Platte Peak." Ascend the top part of the Northwest Ridge Route to the summit of "Lost Platte Peak." Descend the Northwest Ridge Route of "Lost Platte Peak."

*Not to have known,*
*as most have not,*
*either mountain or desert,*
*is not to have known one's self.*

—Joseph Krutch

# chapter two

# Kenosha Mountains

## Introduction

The Kenosha Mountains are the mountains south of the Platte River Mountains. People often get these two ranges confused. It takes a trained eye to distinguish the Kenosha Mountains' twelvers just showing beyond the Platte River Mountains' eleveners as you approach Bailey on U.S. 285. There are six twelvers in the Kenosha Mountains, which is more than half of the Retirement Range's twelvers. It is here that the Retirement Range blooms.

In this chapter, we describe all the Kenosha Mountains' twelvers and selected other peaks. All these summits are in the Pike National Forest and the Lost Creek Wilderness. We describe the summits from northwest to southeast.

Like the boundary of the Platte River Mountains, the Kenosha Mountains' boundary is confusing for such a small range. The Kenosha Mountains' northern boundary is Craig Creek and the North Fork of the South Platte River. The Kenosha Mountains' eastern boundary is the South Platte River. The Kenosha Mountains' southern boundary is Goose Creek, the South Fork of Lost Creek and Long Gulch. The Kenosha Mountains' western boundary is Rock Creek to the 11,660-foot saddle 0.6 mile south of Foster Benchmark and a straight line from this saddle to the 11,540-foot saddle 0.7 mile west of "Platte Peak" at the headwaters of Craig Creek. Thus, we have come full circle. This liberal definition for the Kenosha Mountains includes many lower summits east of the twelvers. A list of all the summits in the Kenosha Mountains is in the Appendix.

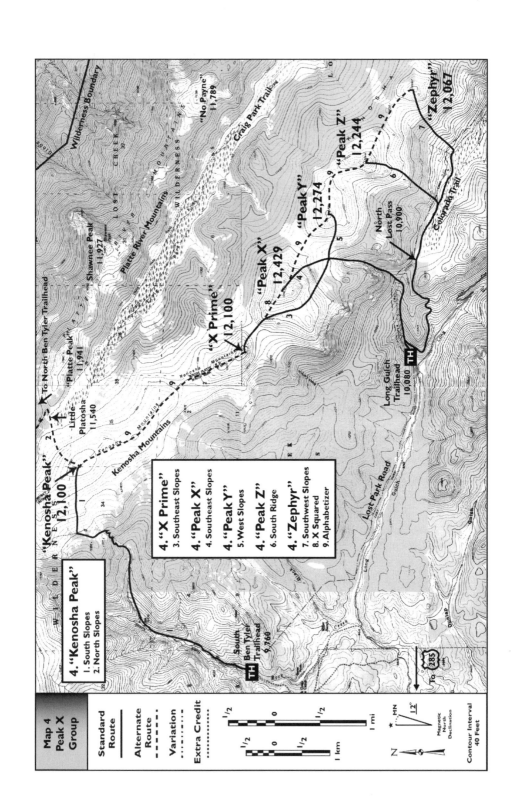

Map 4
Peak X
Group

Standard
Route

Alternate
Route

Variation

Extra Credit

1/2    0    1/2    1 mi

1/2    0    1/2    1 km

N

MN
12°

Magnetic
North
Declination

Contour Interval
40 Feet

"Kenosha Peak"
12,100

4. "Kenosha Peak"
  1. South Slopes
  2. North Slopes

4. "X Prime"
  3. Southeast Slopes

4. "Peak X"
  4. Southeast Slopes

4. "Peak Y"
  5. West Slopes

4. "Peak Z"
  6. South Ridge

4. "Zephyr"
  7. Southwest Slopes
  8. X Squared
  9. Alphabetizer

"X Prime"
12,100

"Peak X"
12,429

"Peak Y"
12,274

"Peak Z"
12,244

"Zephyr"
12,067

North
Lost Pass
10,900

Long Gulch
Trailhead
10,080    TH

South
Ben Tyler
Trailhead
9,760    TH

To North Ben Tyler Trailhead

"Little
Platosha"
11,540

"Platte Peak"
11,941

Shawnee Peak
11,927

"No Payne"
11,789

Wilderness Boundary

Craig Park Trail

Colorado Trail

Kenosha Mountains

Platte River Mountains

Lost Park Road

To 285

# 4. PEAK X GROUP

See map 4, page 20

| | |
|---|---|
| "Kenosha Peak" | 12,100 feet |
| "X Prime" | 12,100 feet |
| "Peak X" | 12,429 feet |
| "Peak Y" | 12,274 feet |
| "Peak Z" | 12,244 feet |
| "Zephyr" | 12,067 feet |

These magnificent peaks form the main ridge of the Kenosha Mountains. They rest in silent splendor between Craig Creek to the north, Long Gulch to the southwest and Lost Creek to the southeast. All these peaks are in the Lost Creek Wilderness. "Peak X" is 5.3 miles southeast of South Twin Cone Peak. The crest of the Kenosha Mountains is above treeline from Platosha to "Zephyr," a distance of 6.7 miles. The Peak X Group combined with the Twin Cone Group in the Platte River Mountains offers 10.0 miles of ridge above treeline. No other ridge in the Retirement Range comes close to matching this grandeur. This intimate, hidden high country is only 40 miles from downtown Denver. Let the magic unfold.

21

## Maps

*Required: Mount Logan, Topaz Mountain*
*Optional: Observatory Rock, Shawnee*

## Trailhead

### Long Gulch Trailhead

This important trailhead is at 10,080 feet and provides access to the south sides of all the peaks in the Peak X Group. If approaching from the east, go 3.0 miles southwest on U.S. 285 from the summit of Kenosha Pass. If approaching from the south, go 1.2 miles northeast on U.S. 285 from the small town of Jefferson. Turn east on Park County 56 (Lost Park Road) and measure from this point.

Go east on Park County 56 and enter the Pike National Forest at 1.9 miles. The road becomes FS 56 at this point. It is still Lost Park Road. Continue southeast on Lost Park Road, stay east (left) at 5.1 miles, pass Rock Creek Road at 7.0 miles, pass Rock Creek at 7.6 miles, continue east and reach the turn for Long Gulch Trailhead at 10.6 miles. Turn northeast (left) onto a short spur road and reach the signed trailhead at 10.7 miles.

This is one of only three trailheads in this book that are over 10,000 feet. Unlike Kenosha Pass Trailhead, you cannot drive north from Long Gulch Trailhead because the Lost Creek Wilderness is just north of the trailhead. This trailhead is sometimes accessible in winter.

*On top of "Kenosha Peak"*

See
map 4,
page 20

# 4. "Kenosha Peak"  12,100 feet

"Kenosha Peak" is 2.4 miles southeast of South Twin Cone Peak. "Kenosha Peak" is the northernmost peak in the Kenosha Mountains and the northwesternmost of six twelvers that form the heart of the Kenosha Mountains. It is 1.0 mile southwest of Platosha, the point where the Kenosha Mountains meet the Platte River Mountains. Many people confuse the Kenosha and Platte River Mountains near Platosha. Ascend "Kenosha Peak" and you will better understand the difference. It has a gentle, rounded summit suitable for lounging.

You can easily reach "Kenosha Peak" from the Ben Tyler Trail starting at either North or South Ben Tyler Trailhead. "Kenosha Peak" is the only peak in the Kenosha Mountains that you can easily approach from U.S. 285 north of the range.

## Routes

### 4.1 South Slopes *Classic*
*From South Ben Tyler TH at 9,760 ft:   94 RP   7.8 mi   2,340 ft   Class 1*

This is the easiest route on "Kenosha Peak" and the easiest route on a Retirement Range twelver. This Class 1 hike lets you sample the Kenosha Mountains without a large effort. Start at South Ben Tyler Trailhead (see Twin Cone Group). Hike 3.1 miles north, east, then north up Rock Creek on the excellent Ben Tyler Trail to treeline at 11,400 feet. You do not need to go all the way to Platosha, the 11,660-foot saddle between South Twin Cone Peak and "Kenosha Peak." Leave the trail at 11,400 feet and hike 0.8 mile east up open slopes to the placid summit. You can easily avoid the few bushes near the trail, and the upper slopes are wide open. From the summit, you can see South Twin Cone to the northwest, the Platte River Mountains' eleveners to the east and the craggy summit of "Peak X" to the southeast. On a clear day, you can see Crestone Needle and Crestone Peak far to the south.

### 4.2 North Slopes

*From North Ben Tyler TH at 8,260 ft: 164 RP    11.6 mi    3,840 ft    Class 2*

This is a longer and slightly rougher hike than the South Slopes Route, but it is a shorter drive if you are coming from Denver. Start at North Ben Tyler Trailhead (see Twin Cone Group) and hike 4.3 miles southwest up the Ben Tyler Trail to a trail junction at 11,000 feet. Turn east (left) onto the Craig Park Trail and hike 0.8 mile to Little Platosha, the 11,540-foot saddle between "Platte Peak" and "Kenosha Peak." Leave the Craig Park Trail here and hike 0.7 mile southwest to the summit (Class 2).

# 4. "X Prime"    12,100 feet

See map 4, page 20

"X Prime" is 2.2 miles southeast of "Kenosha Peak" and 0.8 mile northwest of "Peak X." "X Prime" is the fifth-highest peak in the Kenosha Mountains and has a soft rank. "X Prime" has three small summits. The rocky southeast summit is the highest and is worth a visit. "X Prime" is typically ascended together with "Peak X," but it is an excellent outing by itself.

"X Prime"
12,100

*"X Prime" from the southeast*

### Route

#### 4.3 Southeast Slopes

*From Long Gulch TH at 10,080 ft:     127 RP     6.6 mi     2,580 ft     Class 2*

This is the shortest route on "X Prime." Start at Long Gulch Trailhead and follow the Southeast Slopes Route on "Peak X" to treeline at 11,600 feet. Leave that route and hike 0.7 mile northwest to 12,100 feet in a wonderful open area south of the summit of "Peak X." Descend 0.5 mile north-northwest to the 11,820-foot saddle between "Peak X" and "X Prime." Hike 0.3 mile west-northwest and approach the summit of "X Prime" from the northwest. The highest point is the southeasternmost of three small summits. From the summit, you will appreciate the view of "Peak X." Return the same way. If you descend south from the slopes of "X Prime" or "Peak X," you will find rough, rocky terrain, bushes and dense aspen trees.

See
map 4,
page 20

## 4. "Peak X"     12,429 feet

"Peak X," 5.3 miles southeast of South Twin Cone Peak, is the highest peak in the Kenosha Mountains and the second-highest peak in the Retirement Range. "Peak X" is three feet short of being the highest peak in the Retirement Range; only 12,431-foot Bison Peak tops it. Sometimes called "Knobby Crest," "Peak X" is one of the Retirement Range's Big 4. The peak's stature is amazing. At 12,000 feet, above most Retirement Range peaks, "Peak X" is still almost a mile wide! You can see it from U.S. 285 north of Bailey and from much of South Park. The peak's summit is a rock wonderland, and approaching it can make you feel like an accomplished explorer.

*"Peak X" from "Peak Y"*

## Route

### 4.4 Southeast Slopes *Classic*

*From Long Gulch TH at 10,080 ft:     101 RP     5.0 mi     2,349 ft     Class 2*

This short, purifying tour is the easiest route up "Peak X." Start your hike at Long Gulch Trailhead. The creek northeast of the trailhead comes from the 11,740-foot saddle between "Peak X" and "Peak Y." Cross to the creek's southeast side and hike 0.2 mile northeast on a spur trail to the Colorado Trail and a trail junction. The Colorado Trail crosses the drainage here. For this hike, you do not want to use the Colorado Trail. Where a trail sign indicates the Colorado Trail going south, look sharp and find the Hooper Trail heading east. Follow the Hooper Trail 0.7 mile east as it ascends along the creek's south side. The Topaz Mountain Quadrangle incorrectly shows the Hooper Trail on the creek's north side where there are only bushes. At 10,700 feet on the Hooper Trail, look sharp and find a spur trail going northeast. Leave the Hooper Trail and hike 0.9 mile north-northeast along the creek's east side on this useful spur trail to treeline at 11,600 feet.

At treeline, "Peak X" is 0.6 mile northwest and "Peak Y" is 0.5 mile east. There are many bushes in the 11,740-foot saddle between these two peaks. To avoid most of them, look for a suitable place, leave the spur trail, cross to the creek's west side and hike 0.5 mile northwest to 12,200 feet (Class 2). Only the broad summit plateau remains. Hike 0.2 mile west between the Xebec Towers to the south and the summit rocks to the north. The summit rocks offer several outcrops to choose from, and the highest point may not be immediately obvious. It is the central and northernmost formation. It will be obvious when you reach the highest point. The views are expansive.

*At treeline on "Peak X"*

*High on "Peak X"*

See
map 4,
page 20

## 4. "Peak Y"      12,274 feet

"Peak Y" is 1.0 mile southeast of "Peak X." Continuing the fine tradition of "Peak X," "Peak Y" is the second-highest peak in the Kenosha Mountains and the sixth-highest peak in the Retirement Range. Although "Peak Y" is a little lower and smaller than the mighty "Peak X," it is still grand. It is also easier to ascend than "Peak X."

*"Peak Y" from North Tarryall Peak*

26

**Route**

### 4.5 West Slopes *Classic*

*From Long Gulch TH at 10,080 ft:*      *88 RP*    *4.6 mi*   *2,194 ft*   *Class 2*

This is the easiest route up "Peak Y." Start at Long Gulch Trailhead and follow the Southeast Slopes Route on "Peak X" to treeline at 11,600 feet. Leave the spur trail here and hike 0.5 mile east to the summit. Approach the highest point from the south. Perhaps, on "Peak Y," you will no longer ask why.

## 4. "Peak Z"    12,244 feet

"Peak Z" is 0.7 mile southeast of "Peak Y." To complete the Kenosha alphabet, "Peak Z" is the third-highest peak in the Kenosha Mountains and the seventh-highest peak in the Retirement Range. "Peak Z" is a little farther from Long Gulch Trailhead than either "Peak X" or "Peak Y," and you will feel more isolated here. For many, that is sufficient reason to choose this hike.

27

See map 4, page 20

*"Peak Z" from the west*

**Route**

### 4.6 South Ridge *Classic*

*From Long Gulch TH at 10,080 ft:*      *124 RP*    *6.4 mi*   *2,424 ft*   *Class 2*

This is the easiest route up "Peak Z." It is a tougher and slightly longer hike than either "Peak X" or "Peak Y." It is worth it. Start at Long Gulch Trailhead, cross to the creek's southeast side and hike 0.2 mile northeast on a spur trail to the Colorado Trail and a trail junction. For this hike, you do use part of the Colorado Trail. Where a trail sign indicates the Colorado Trail going south, follow the Colorado Trail 1.3 miles south then east to a 10,900-foot saddle at the headwaters of the North Fork of Lost Creek. This is North Lost Pass. Continue 0.7 mile east-southeast on the Colorado Trail as it descends gently into the North Fork of Lost Creek. At 10,760 feet, you are directly below the south ridge of "Peak Z" and less than a mile from the summit. Your fun has just begun.

Leave the Colorado Trail and begin your ascent to the heights. Hike 0.5 mile northeast to treeline at 11,500 feet. For the easiest route, stay to the east of the ridge crest. From treeline, hike 0.5 mile north-northeast to the summit. Stay east of some rock outcrops along the way. The highest point may surprise you. Actually standing on the highest point requires you to overcome a few Class 2+ moves. The spirit of the Retirement Range is on top of "Peak Z." We hope that you can find it.

*On top of "Peak Z"*

## 4. "Zephyr"    12,067 feet

See
map 4,
page 20
"Zephyr" is 1.0 mile southeast of "Peak Z." It is the most remote summit in the Peak X Group and requires the longest hike for a single peak in this group. As always, the greatest effort takes you to the most privileged position. The west wind will help you get there.

"Zephyr"
12,067

*Hiking from "Peak Z" toward "Zephyr"*

## Route
### 4.7 Southwest Slopes *Classic*
*From Long Gulch TH at 10,080 ft:      123 RP     7.4 mi     2,267 ft     Class 2*

This is the easiest route up "Zephyr." Start at Long Gulch Trailhead and follow the South Ridge Route on "Peak Z" to 10,760 feet in the North Fork of Lost Creek. Continue another 0.6 mile east-southeast on the Colorado Trail. After this short stroll, you are still at 10,760 feet. Leave the Colorado Trail, hike 0.5 mile northeast to treeline at 11,400 feet and hike 0.4 mile east to the highest point of "Zephyr."

This is a special, peaceful place. If you quit asking why on "Peak Y" and found the spirit of the Retirement Range on "Peak Z," then you may feel filamentary breezes flow through you on "Zephyr."

# 4. Peak X Group Combinations
### 4.8 X Squared
*From Long Gulch TH at 10,080 ft:      146 RP     6.7 mi     2,909 ft     Class 2*

See map 4, page 20

This is the easiest way to ascend "Peak X" and "X Prime" together. Start at Long Gulch Trailhead and ascend the Southeast Slopes Route on "Peak X." From the summit of "Peak X," descend 0.6 mile northwest to the 11,820-foot saddle between "Peak X" and "X Prime." Hike 0.3 mile west-northwest and approach the summit of "X Prime" from the northwest. The highest point is the southeasternmost of three small summits. Descend the Southeast Slopes Route of "X Prime."

### 4.9 Alphabetizer *Classic*

| | | | | |
|---|---|---|---|---|
| *From Long Gulch TH at 10,080 ft:* | *196 RP* | *8.2 mi* | *3,644 ft* | *Class 2* |
| *With "X Prime":* | *240 RP* | *9.9 mi* | *4,204 ft* | *Class 2* |
| *With "Kenosha Peak":* | *272 RP* | *12.8 mi* | *4,244 ft* | *Class 2* |

This is the easiest way to ascend Peaks X, Y and Z and "Zephyr" together. This wonderful high ridge is an obvious place to stretch your legs between the summits. The ridge does not drop below treeline between "Zephyr" and "Kenosha Peak." We cannot stay on the summits forever, but sometimes we can choose to stay as long as possible.

You can do this traverse in either direction, but it is more aesthetically pleasing to ascend higher and higher summits toward mighty "Peak X." Start at Long Gulch Trailhead and ascend the Southwest Slopes Route on "Zephyr." From the summit of "Zephyr," hike 0.3 mile northwest to the 11,730-foot saddle between "Zephyr" and "Peak Z," then hike 0.7 mile west-northwest to "Peak Z." From the summit of "Peak Z," hike 0.4 mile north-northwest to the 11,940-foot saddle between "Peak Z" and "Peak Y," then hike 0.4 mile west to "Peak Y." From the summit of "Peak Y," hike 0.4 mile northwest to the 11,740-foot saddle between "Peak Y" and "Peak X," then hike 0.5 mile west-northwest to "Peak X." Descend the Southeast Slopes Route on "Peak X."

If you choose to continue from "Peak X" to "X Prime," you will complete a marvelous Kenosha caper. With a vehicle shuttle between Long Gulch Trailhead and South Ben Tyler Trailhead, you can continue from "X Prime" to "Kenosha Peak" and complete a Kenosha twelver sweep.

## 5. WINDY PEAK GROUP

| | |
|---|---|
| **Windy Peak** | **11,970 feet** |
| **Buffalo Peak** | **11,589 feet** |
| **The Castle** | **9,691 feet** |

*See map 5A, page 32*

*See map 5B, page 40*

These peaks anchor the Kenosha Mountains' southeastern end. Windy and Buffalo are in the Lost Creek Wilderness and are the Kenosha Mountains' highest eleveners. The Castle is between Windy and Buffalo on the eastern boundary of the Lost Creek Wilderness. East of these peaks, the mountains decrease in height to the South Platte River, rise in a salute called the Rampart Range, then fall away to Colorado's eastern plains. From Buffalo's summit, you can see downtown Denver 37 miles to the northeast. You can see Buffalo and Windy from Interstate 25 south of Denver. You can catch peekaboo views of the Castle from U.S. 285.

### Maps

*Required: Windy Peak, Green Mountain*
*Optional: Topaz Mountain, Cheesman Lake*

## Trailheads
### Lost Park Trailhead

This trailhead is at 9,980 feet and provides access to Windy Peak's west ridge. Go to Lost Pass Trailhead (see North Tarryall Group). Do not confuse Lost Pass Trailhead and Lost Park Trailhead. From Lost Pass, continue east-southeast on Lost Park Road for 6.3 miles to Lost Park Trailhead. The signed trailhead is at the end of Lost Park Road in a stand of trees just west of Lost Park Campground. The trailhead and campground are near the confluence of the North and South Forks of Lost Creek. The Lost Creek Wilderness is on three sides of Lost Park Trailhead. This is a special place; many scintillating hikes start here.

This trailhead is not accessible in winter. The Forest Service gates Lost Park Road below the two switchbacks on the northwest side of Lost Pass. This gate is 7.7 miles from Lost Park Trailhead. This is a seasonal closure and the Forest Service does not usually open the road until June 15. For information about the state of this gate, call the South Park Ranger District at (719) 836-2031.

### Rolling Creek Trailhead

This trailhead is at 8,340 feet and provides access to Windy Peak's north and east ridges and Buffalo's west ridge. Go to Bailey on U.S. 285. Bailey is 28.0 miles west of the U.S. 285–CO 470 junction in southwest Denver. On the east edge of Bailey, turn east onto Park County 68 and measure from this point.

Go east on Park County 68 (paved), cross to the south side of the North Fork of the South Platte at mile 0.5 and enter the Pike National Forest at mile 1.0. The road is still Park County 68, but it is now also FS 543. Continue southeast on FS 543. The pavement ends at mile 1.3, but the road is still excellent. Turn south (right) at mile 5.1 and stay on FS 543 (Wellington Lake Road). Go straight (right) on Wellington Lake Road at mile 6.8 and reach a spur road leading to Rolling Creek Trailhead at mile 8.0. The Colorado Trail crosses FS 543 at this point. Turn west (right) onto the spur road (also the Colorado Trail), go west then south and reach the signed trailhead at mile 8.25. From this trailhead, the Rolling Creek Trail goes south and the Colorado Trail goes north.

In winter, you can usually drive to the junction with the spur road at mile 8.0. Park on the west side of FS 543 and walk 0.25 mile west to the trailhead.

### Wellington Lake Trailhead

This trailhead is at 8,020 feet and provides access to the Castle and Buffalo's northeast slopes. You can approach Wellington Lake from the north or east.

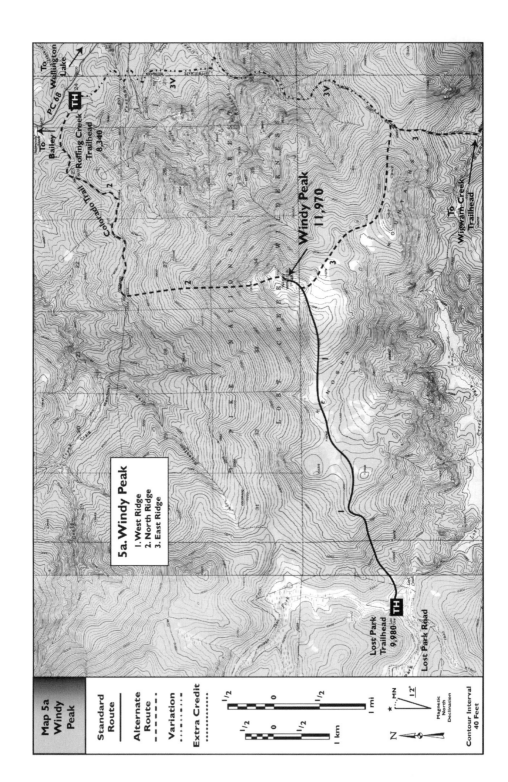

Map 5a
Windy
Peak

Standard
Route

Alternate
Route

Variation

Extra Credit

5a. Windy Peak

1. West Ridge
2. North Ridge
3. East Ridge

Windy Peak
11,970

To
Bailey

To Wellington
Lake

PC 68

Rolling Creek
Trailhead
8,340

TH

Colorado Trail

To
Wigwam Creek
Trailhead

PIKE NATIONAL FOREST

LOST CREEK WILDERNESS

KENOSHA

Lost Park
Trailhead
9,980

TH

Lost Park Road

3V

3V

1/2          0          1/2          1 mi

1/2     0     1/2     1 km

N

MN
12°
Magnetic
North
Declination

Contour Interval
40 Feet

For the northern approach, follow the directions for Rolling Creek Trailhead to the spur road at mile 8.0. Continue south on FS 543 (Wellington Lake Road), pass the Jefferson County Outdoor Education School at mile 8.8, pass Wellington Lake's northeast side at mile 10.4 and reach the entrance to the Castle Mountain Recreation Company at mile 11.0. Turn northwest (right), and stop at the office.

For the scenic eastern approach, go to Pine Junction on U.S. 285 and go 13.2 miles south on Jefferson County 126 through Pine and Buffalo Creek, turn west (right) onto FS 550 and measure from this point. Go west on FS 550, pass Buffalo Campground at mile 4.8, pass Meadows Group Campground at mile 5.0 and go straight (left) onto FS 543 at mile 5.3. Go west on FS 543, pass Green Mountain Campground at mile 6.9 and reach the FS 543–560 junction on Wellington Lake's east side at mile 7.9. There is a good view of Buffalo and the Castle from here. Go 50 yards north (right) on FS 543 to the Castle Mountain Recreation Company, turn northwest (left) and stop at the office.

33

Wellington Lake and the land around it are privately owned. You can drive past the lake on the Forest Service roads, but the Castle Mountain Recreation Company controls access to the lake. It is open from April through October and charges $4.50/day for adults, $3/day for children under 12 and $3/day for seniors 60 and up. Children under five are free. For more information, call (303) 838-5496.

Pay your fees and go 0.6 mile northwest along the lakeshore to camp area 1 on the lake's northwest shore. If you want to hike around the Castle's north side, park here. If you want to hike around the Castle's south side, continue 0.5 mile south along the lake's west shore to camp area 4 and park. In winter, you can usually drive to Wellington Lake.

## Stoney Pass Trailhead

This trailhead is at 8,562 feet and provides access to Buffalo Peak's northeast side. From the entrance to the Castle Mountain Recreation Company (see Wellington Lake Trailhead), go 50 yards south on FS 543 to the FS 543–560 junction on the east side of Wellington Lake and measure from this point. Go south on FS 560 (Stoney Pass Road) and cross the Wellington Lake Dam at mile 0.3. From here, there is a good view of the Castle's southeast side and Buffalo Peak's northeast side. Continue southeast on the rougher FS 560 and reach Stoney Pass at mile 2.4. This is the trailhead. Park right at the pass on the west side of FS 560.

This trailhead is not usually accessible in winter. FS 560 over Stoney Pass is not plowed, but the road is not gated. Four-wheel-drive vehicles can often reach Stoney Pass in winter.

### Wigwam Creek Trailhead

This trailhead is at 8,160 feet and provides access to Windy Peak's east ridge and Buffalo Peak's west ridge. You can approach this trailhead from the north or east.

For the northern approach, go to Stoney Pass Trailhead and measure from this point. Go south on FS 560 to Webster Park at mile 2.3. There is a nice view of Buffalo Peak from here. Continue south on FS 560, turn west (right) onto FS 545 (unmarked) at mile 3.3 and enjoy an excellent view of Buffalo Peak. For Buffalo's Southeast Slopes Route, park here at 8,213 feet.

For the eastern approach, go to Woodland Park on U.S. 24. Go 23 miles north on CO 67 to Deckers, go straight (left) onto Jefferson County 126 and cross the South Platte River. Go 2.6 miles west on Jefferson County 126, turn west (left) onto FS 211 and measure from this point. You can also reach this junction by traveling 12.0 miles south on Jefferson County 126 from Buffalo Creek (see Wellington Lake Trailhead). Go west on FS 211 and turn west (right) onto FS 560 (Stoney Pass Road) at mile 3.0. Go west on FS 560, turn north (right) at mile 4.5 and turn west (left) onto FS 545 (unmarked) at mile 6.7. For Buffalo's Southeast Slopes Route, park here at 8,213 feet.

From the FS 560–545 junction, go 1.3 miles west on FS 545 to Wigwam Creek Trailhead. There is no parking right at the trailhead, but there are two parking areas nearby. The lower parking area is 100 yards east of the trailhead, and the upper parking area is 100 yards northeast.

*Windy Peak from the northwest*

This trailhead is usually not accessible in winter. However, the elevation is not great here and this sunny area is available much of the year, especially if you use the eastern approach.

# 5. Windy Peak    11,970 feet

See map 5A, page 32

Windy Peak is 10.0 miles southeast of "Peak X" and 7.4 miles south-southeast of Bailey. You can see Windy Peak to the south as you approach Bailey on U.S. 285. Windy Peak is the highest elevener in the Retirement Range and one of the range's Big 4. Windy Peak's isolated position gives it a lot of power. Although it just misses 12,000 feet, Windy Peak has a huge summit area. If you cut the peak off at 11,500 feet, the resulting plateau would measure 1.3 by 1.4 miles! Windy Peak offers a choice of routes and is harder to ascend than "Peak X." There are no trails near the summit. Walking across Windy Peak's spacious summit plateau is an activity tailored for those with vision, not those just wanting a view.

35

## Routes

### 5.1 West Ridge *Classic*
*From Lost Park TH at 9,980 ft:*        *193 RP    8.0 mi    2,538 ft    Class 2*

This is the easiest route on Windy Peak, but it is not an easy hike. This rough, rewarding hike is an off-trail, navigational challenge from trailhead to treeline. Start at Lost Park Trailhead. Windy Peak's large mass is east of the trailhead, but you can see only the peak's lower slopes. Let the challenge begin.

From the trailhead, hike 0.2 mile east and cross the North Fork of Lost Creek en route. Hike 0.2 mile northeast up an open meadow and enter the Lost Creek Wilderness. Hike 0.1 mile north to the top of the meadow at 10,200 feet. Enter the trees and hike 0.7 mile northeast up a rough slope to a slight ridge at 11,200 feet. You are now on the beginning of Windy Peak's long, broad west ridge. The slope angle is less here, but your navigational challenge increases. Ascending slightly, hike 0.4 mile east on the north side of Point 11,414. Descending slightly, hike 0.5 mile northeast to a broad 11,246-foot saddle. Ascending slightly, hike 0.75 mile east to 11,400 feet. You are now at the base of Windy Peak's upper massif, and route finding is easier.

From 11,400 feet, hike 0.2 mile east to treeline at 11,600 feet. From here, you still cannot see Windy Peak's summit. Persevere and hike 0.4 mile east to Point 11,900. This is a false summit, but at least you can see the main summit! Descend 0.3 mile northeast to an 11,740-foot saddle and hike 0.25 mile northeast past some rock outcrops to Windy Peak's summit. The highpoint is craggy and often windy.

### 5.2 North Ridge

*From Rolling Creek TH at 8,340 ft:    190 RP    9.4 mi    3,630 ft    Class 2*

This adventurous route is longer than Windy Peak's West Ridge Route. You can use the Colorado Trail for part of your ascent, but the bushwhack from the trail to the summit is rough and you start at a low trailhead.

Start at Rolling Creek Trailhead where the Rolling Creek Trail goes south and the Colorado Trail goes north. For this hike, you want the Colorado Trail. Hike 2.8 miles generally west on the Colorado Trail as it ascends steadily to a trail junction at 9,300 feet. From this junction, the Payne Creek Trail descends northwest and the Colorado Trail continues west. Leave the Colorado Trail at the Payne Creek–Colorado Trail junction and hike 0.8 mile south through dense trees to 10,400 feet, where Windy Peak's north ridge becomes distinct. Hike 0.6 mile south up this rough ridge to treeline at 11,500 feet. This ridge is the route's crux, as there are large boulders in the trees. To minimize difficulties, stay on the ridge's west side. From treeline, you can enjoy the summit ride. Hike 0.5 mile south up open ground to the highest point.

### 5.3 East Ridge

*From Wigwam Creek TH at 8,160 ft:  251 RP  14.9 mi  4,798 ft  Class 2*

This is a long route up Windy Peak. You use the Wigwam and Rolling Creek Trails to get high on the peak's east side. Then you must bushwhack to treeline. Start at Wigwam Gulch Trailhead, hike 0.15 mile west on an old

Windy Peak
11,970

North Ridge

*Windy Peak from the east*

road and descend to Wigwam Creek at 8,140 feet. This is the route's low point and the lowest point on any Kenosha Mountains hike in this book. Before the road crosses Wigwam Creek, leave it and turn west (right) onto the Wigwam Trail. Hike 3.0 miles west on the Wigwam Trail into the Lost Creek Wilderness, crossing Wigwam Creek four times en route, to a trail junction in Wigwam Park at 9,500 feet. At this trail junction, the Goose Creek Trail goes south in search of Lost Creek. Continue west on the Wigwam Trail for another 0.6 mile to a second trail junction at 9,620 feet. Leave the Wigwam Trail and hike 1.2 miles north on the Rolling Creek Trail to the 10,660-foot saddle between Windy Peak and Buffalo Peak. This is the highest that any trail gets on Windy Peak. The introduction is over. Now for your bushwhack.

37

Leave the comfort of the Rolling Creek Trail, plunge into the forest and hike 0.5 mile west up a steep slope to Point 11,412. Continue another 0.5 mile west to Point 11,517. From here, you will understand this route's challenge. You are only 453 feet below the summit, but you still have work to do. Descend 0.25 mile north-northwest to a 11,235-foot saddle, hike 0.4 mile northwest and ascend a southeast-facing slope to Point 11,540. Now your summit ride is at hand. Hike 0.6 mile northwest on open ground to 11,600 feet, then hike 0.25 mile north-northeast past some rock outcrops to the highest point.

Ascending the North Ridge Route and descending the East Ridge Route makes a tough Tour de Windy. For this tour, you will need a vehicle shuttle between Rolling Creek and Wigwam Creek Trailheads.

### 5.3V Variation
*From Rolling Creek TH at 8,340 ft:    253 RP    15.0 mi    4,858 ft    Class 1*

You can reach the 10,660-foot saddle between Windy and Buffalo Peaks from the north. This effort is equivalent to the Wigwam Creek approach except that your drive from Bailey will be shorter. Start at Rolling Creek Trailhead and hike 5.0 miles south on the Rolling Creek Trail to the saddle, crossing Freeman Creek, North Rolling Creek and Rolling Creek en route. Join the upper route in the saddle.

## 5. Buffalo Peak    11,589 feet

See map 5B, page 40

Buffalo Peak is 4.4 miles southeast of Windy Peak on the eastern edge of the Retirement Range's high peaks. You can see Buffalo's large mass from many vantages to the east. You can also see Buffalo to the south from U.S. 285 north of Bailey. Buffalo Peak has a named benchmark on its summit called Freeman Peak, and some people call this peak "Buffalo-Freeman." Buffalo's main claim to fame is that it is the highest peak in Jefferson County. Buffalo is the only peak in the Retirement Range that is a county summit.

Buffalo Peak
11,589

*Buffalo Peak from the southeast*

Because of this stature, you might expect to see more hikers on Buffalo than on other Retirement Range peaks. However, like Windy, Buffalo has no easy route to its summit. The trailheads east of the peak are low, and Buffalo has a reputation for providing a tough ascent. Buffalo is easier to ascend than Windy, but Buffalo's craggy summit is still reserved for dedicated hikers.

## Routes
### 5.4 Northeast Slopes
*From Stoney Pass TH at 8,562 ft:*      *155 RP*    *5.2 mi*    *3,027 ft*    *Class 2*

This is the easiest route on Buffalo. The hike is completely off-trail and is stark in its simplicity. Start at Stoney Pass Trailhead and bushwhack 2.3 miles southwest up a seemingly unrelenting slope to 11,400 feet. The slope does relent at 11,400 feet, and Buffalo's summit ride is short. Hike 0.3 mile west to the highest point, which is the westernmost of two rock outcrops. Approach the summit from the north.

To the northwest, you can see Grays Peak, the highest peak in both Clear Creek and Summit Counties. Far to the north, you can just see Longs Peak, the highest peak in Boulder County. From the summit, you can survey Jefferson County to the east. It is all below you. To the southeast you can see Thunder Butte, the highest peak in Douglas County. To the south, you can see the Pikes Peak massif, which holds the highest points in El Paso and Teller

Counties. These county summits salute your ascent of Buffalo, the highest peak in Jefferson County.

## 5.5 Southeast Slopes

*From FS 560–545 junction at 8,213 ft:164 RP    5.2 mi    3,376 ft    Class 2*

This route has a little more elevation gain than the Northeast Slopes Route, but it is mostly south facing. Buffalo's upper northeast slopes hold deep snow well into spring, and this snow can turn your strenuous bushwhack into an even more memorable day. In spring, consider this route; Gerry ascended it in February 1983, as his last Colorado training hike before climbing Mount Everest.

Park at the FS 560–545 junction at 8,213 feet (see Wigwam Creek Trailhead). From here, you have a great view of the route. As you measure the slope with your eye, know one thing: It is tougher than it appears. You can see Point 9,870 and a small ridge above it from the starting point. Read the description below and plan your route accordingly.

Like the Northeast Slopes Route, this hike is completely off-trail and is stark in its simplicity. Hike 1.0 mile northwest to 9,000 feet. Hike 0.6 mile northwest to 10,000 feet, staying west of Point 9,870 en route. Hike 0.6 mile northwest to 11,200 feet, staying west of a small ridge en route. At 11,200 feet, the slope relents. Hike 0.4 mile west-northwest to the summit, which is the westernmost of two rock outcrops. Approach the summit from the north. Return via Mount Everest.

## 5.6 West Ridge *Classic*

*From Wigwam Creek TH at 8,160 ft:  196 RP    14.5 mi    3,549 ft    Class 2*

This route on Buffalo allows you to gain some of the elevation on trails, but it is a much longer hike than the Northeast or Southeast Slopes Routes. Start at Wigwam Creek Trailhead and follow Windy Peak's East Ridge Route to the 10,660-foot saddle between Windy and Buffalo. Leave Rolling Creek Trail here, hike 0.8 mile east and contour on the north side of Point 11,332. The ridge ahead is level and may test your route-finding skills. Hike 0.5 mile west across the flats, contour 0.4 mile east-southeast on the north side of Point 11,380, and hike 0.6 mile east then east-southeast along Buffalo's rough upper west ridge to the summit.

Ascending the West Ridge Route and descending the Southeast Slopes Route makes a nifty and comprehensive Tour de Buffalo. At 8,800 feet on your descent of the Southeast Slopes Route, descend 0.5 mile south to FS 545 and walk 0.7 mile west on that road to return to Wigwam Creek Trailhead. This tour requires a vehicle shuttle between Wigwam Creek and Stoney Pass Trailheads.

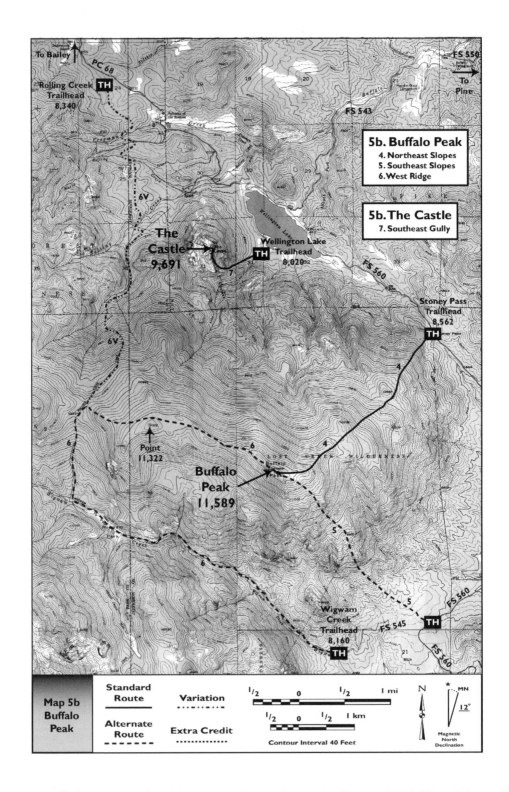

To Bailey
PC 68
Rolling Creek
Trailhead
8,340
FS 543
FS 550
To Pine

6V

The
Castle
9,691

Wellington Lake
Trailhead
8,020

FS 560

Stoney Pass
Trailhead
8,562

6V

Point
11,322

Buffalo
Peak
11,589

LOST CREEK WILDERNESS

Wigwam
Creek
Trailhead
8,160

FS 545

FS 560

**5b. Buffalo Peak**
4. Northeast Slopes
5. Southeast Slopes
6. West Ridge

**5b. The Castle**
7. Southeast Gully

| Map 5b Buffalo Peak | Standard Route | Variation | | | N |
|---|---|---|---|---|---|
| | Alternate Route | Extra Credit | | | |

Contour Interval 40 Feet

½  0  ½  1 mi
½  0  ½  1 km

MN
12°
Magnetic
North
Declination

### 5.6V Variation
*From Rolling Creek TH at 8,340 ft:    198 RP    14.6 mi    3,609 ft    Class 1*

You can reach the 10,660-foot saddle between Windy and Buffalo Peaks from the north. This effort is equivalent to the Wigwam Creek approach except that your drive from Bailey will be shorter. Start at Rolling Creek Trailhead and hike 5.0 miles south on the Rolling Creek Trail to the saddle, crossing Freeman Creek, North Rolling Creek and Rolling Creek en route. Join the upper route in the saddle.

# 5. The Castle    9,691 feet

The Castle is 3.2 miles east-northeast of Windy Peak and 2.6 miles north-northwest of Buffalo Peak. The Castle is a rugged, rocky peak that rises 0.5 mile west of the western shore of popular Wellington Lake. This amazing peak is on the boundary of the Lost Creek Wilderness, and it is a good sentinel for the solitude that exists there. The Castle harbors dozens of towers, sweeping granite walls, convoluted canyons and secret hanging gardens.

41

See map 5B, page 40

Visitors to Wellington Lake gaze at the Castle's ragged ramparts as they play by the water's side. Few attempt to climb the Castle, and fewer still reach the Castle's highest point. There is a good reason for this: The Castle is a technical climb. Although the Castle is harder than the other peaks in this book, it is a significant, named, ranked peak in the Lost Creek Wilderness. It is well known, and we include it in this guide for completeness. The following route description will help those with the requisite skills to reach the top and, we hope, deter casual hikers from making an attempt.

## Route
### 5.7 Southeast Gully *Classic*
*From Wellington Lake TH at 8,020 ft: 140 RP    2.0 mi    1,671 ft    Class 5.4*

This is the easiest route on the Castle and the hardest climb in this book. Hikers without technical climbing skills should avoid this ascent. For rock climbers, though, the ascent can be very rewarding. The Castle is a complicated peak, and it is a good idea to preview the route prior to charging upward. You can get an unobstructed view of most of the route from the Wellington Lake Dam south of the entrance station. The Castle's steep, broken east face is not the route. Look for a large, dramatic, freestanding rock tower on the peak's south ridge. The route ascends a broken gully system between this tower and other large towers to the northeast. The lower part of this gully heads northwest, and the better-defined upper part of the gully heads north between the Castle's two summits. You can see the Castle's eastern summit from Wellington Lake, but the mountain's summit is the more reclusive western summit. During your inspection, also notice some detached, lower cliffs southeast of the summit towers.

*The Castle from the southeast*

Start at Wellington Lake Trailhead. Go south along the lake's west shore to the end of the road and park. Hike west through the Boy Scout Camp and continue 0.1 mile west to the end of a faint road. The introduction is over. Get on the south (left) side of a gully and hike west into the forest. Avoid any temptation to hike straight toward the peak; instead, head for a spot on the ridge well south of the peak. In particular, stay well to the south (left) of the detached, lower cliffs. The route steepens into a challenging slope that will test your hiking skills. As you approach the peak's south ridge, angle to the north to avoid some small cliffs on the south ridge. Aim for the base of the large, dramatic, freestanding rock tower on the peak's south ridge that you identified during your inspection. Hike up to the base of this tower.

From the base of the tower, hike north under the sweeping cliffs above, pass under a steep chimney system and look for an easier angled gully system. There is a large but faded painted arrow pointing upward at the bottom of the correct gully. Even without the arrow, you should be able to identify the correct gully as it is the path of least resistance through the otherwise sweeping cliffs. When ready, begin the technical ascent.

Step onto the rock and climb 15 feet to a two-foot-wide ledge below an imposing chimney (Class 3). To avoid the chimney, walk 15 feet north on the ledge. Climb 20 feet up the rock wall using a south-facing crack (Class 5.4). This 20 feet is one of the route's cruxes. Climb south on a higher ledge over a tiny arch and regain the gully above the imposing chimney (Class 4).

Climb 40 feet up the now easier gully system to a large tree (Class 4). Climb 10 feet above the tree to lower-angled terrain (Class 3).

Climb up the gully system following the path of least resistance. Climb a Class 4 headwall and continue upward on interesting Class 3 scrambling. When the gully bends to the north, follow it. Occasionally, you will have to look sharp to find the easiest route. Higher in the gully you will need to scramble over and between many large boulders. Above the boulders, ground reappears and you will emerge into a flat hanging garden between four summits. The garden is complete with large trees. Hike to the garden's northern end. The lower eastern summit is a simple Class 3 scramble from here, and you may choose to climb the east peak for the views it offers both of Wellington Lake and of the higher western summit. The view of the higher western summit is discouraging. Prepare for a surprise finish.

43

From the garden's northern end, hike and scramble to the base of the western summit's east wall. Climb 20 feet up a tree that is right next to the vertical rock wall. When the rock angles away from the tree, leave the tree and climb 20 feet up a crack to a smaller, higher tree (Class 3). Climb 15 feet above the higher tree into a small notch where you can peer west to the rest of the Castle's ramparts and beyond to Windy Peak. You are close. From just east of the notch, climb south up an eight-foot wall (Class 5.4). Scamper 15 feet south to the highest point (Class 2+). The Castle is yours.

*Wilderness made man but*
*    man cannot make wilderness.*
*He can only spare it.*

—David Brower

# chapter three

# Tarryall Mountains

## Introduction

The Tarryall Mountains are south of the Kenosha Mountains. The Tarryall Mountains include Bison Peak, the highest peak in the Retirement Range. The Tarryall Mountains' other twelver, McCurdy Mountain, is perhaps the finest peak in the Retirement Range. It is here that the Retirement Range reaches full flower. You cannot easily see Bison or McCurdy from civilization, and this makes them even more pristine. Both Bison and McCurdy are in the heart of the Lost Creek Wilderness. On these summits, you will feel free.

In this chapter we describe all the Tarryall Mountains' twelvers and selected other peaks. All these summits are in the Pike National Forest, and five are in the Lost Creek Wilderness. We describe the summits from northwest to southeast.

The Tarryall Mountains' boundary is convoluted. The range's northern boundary is Long Gulch, the South Fork of Lost Creek, Lost Creek and Goose Creek. The range's eastern boundary is the South Platte River. The range's southern boundary is Tarryall Creek. The Tarryall Mountains' western boundary is Rock Creek. A list of all the summits in the Tarryall Mountains is in the Appendix.

## 6. NORTH TARRYALL GROUP

| | |
|---|---|
| **North Tarryall Peak** | **11,902 feet** |
| **Topaz Mountain** | **11,762 feet** |

See
map 6,
page 46

These elevens form the northwest end of the Tarryall Mountains. They are 4 miles south of the peaks in the Peak X Group. They are not visible from U.S. 285 or from points east of the Retirement Range. You can see North

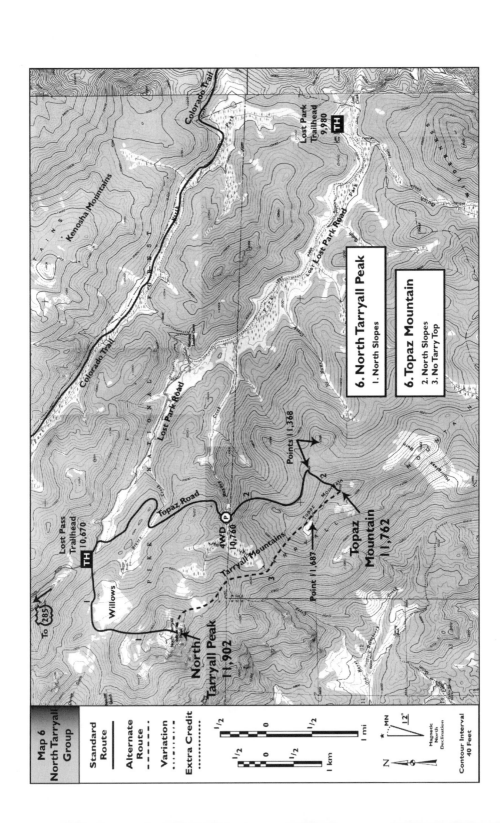

Map 6
North Tarryall
Group

Standard
Route

Alternate
Route

Variation

Extra Credit

6. North Tarryall Peak
1. North Slopes

6. Topaz Mountain
2. North Slopes
3. No Tarry Top

North
Tarryall Peak
11,902

Topaz
Mountain
11,762

Point 11,687

Points 11,368

Tarryall Mountains

Topaz Road

Lost Park Road

Lost Park Road

Lost Pass Trailhead
10,670

Lost Park
Trailhead
9,980

Colorado Trail

Colorado Trail

Kenosha Mountains

4WD

Willows

To 285

Contour Interval
40 Feet

1/2    0    1/2    1 mi

1/2    0    1/2    1 km

N

MN

12°

Magnetic
North
Declination

Tarryall and Topaz from South Park and along the Tarryall Road. Obscure to some, sacred to others, both these peaks have rocky summits that afford you expansive views. Sadly, neither peak is in the Lost Creek Wilderness.

## Maps
*Required: Topaz Mountain*
*Optional: Observatory Rock*

## Trailhead
### Lost Pass Trailhead
This trailhead is at 10,670 feet and provides access to the north sides of North Tarryall Peak and Topaz Mountain. Follow the directions for Long Gulch Trailhead (see Peak X Group). From the turn for Long Gulch Trailhead at 10.6 miles, continue southeast on Lost Park Road, pass a Forest Service gate at 11.6 miles, climb through two switchbacks and reach Lost Pass at 13.0 miles. There are no signs here, but this is the trailhead. Park on the south side of the road. Lost Pass separates the Kenosha and Tarryall Mountains and is the headwaters of Lost Creek.

Lost Pass Trailhead is this book's highest trailhead and one of only three in the book that are over 10,000 feet. This trailhead is not accessible in winter. The Forest Service gates Lost Park Road below the two switchbacks on the northwest side of Lost Pass. This gate is 1.4 miles from Lost Pass, and many parties choose to walk the extra distance. This is a seasonal closure, and the Forest Service does not usually open the road until June 15. For information about the state of this gate, call the South Park Ranger District at (719) 836-2031.

# 6. North Tarryall Peak    11,902 feet

See
map 6,
page 46

North Tarryall Peak is 3.9 miles south of "Peak X" and 5.4 miles north of Tarryall Reservoir. The well-named peak anchors the northwest end of the Tarryall Mountains and has a rugged, rocky summit. The peak is especially striking when you view it from the Tarryall Road to the south. The peak is only 1.3 miles southwest of Lost Pass, and you can easily reach it from there.

## Route
### 6.1 North Slopes
*From Lost Pass TH at 10,670 ft:*       *89 RP*    *3.6 mi*    *1,232 ft*   *Class 2*
This is the easiest route on North Tarryall Peak. The route is short but this stiff bushwhack slows the swift, especially in winter. Start at Lost Pass Trailhead and hike 0.3 mile southwest up a slope to the edge of a large meadow at 11,000 feet. You can see the peak 1.0 mile southwest above the

North Tarryall Peak
11,902

48

*North Tarryall from Eagle Rock*

meadow, but a direct ascent is not reasonable due to the many bushes that inhabit the meadow. To avoid the bushes, hike 0.6 mile west-northwest then west along the meadow's north edge to a broad, wooded, 11,140-foot saddle. There is a use trail along the meadow's edge to help you. Many animals have had the same idea. From the saddle, hike 0.7 mile south to treeline at 11,800 feet. Your summit ride is short but sweet. Hike 0.2 mile south, staying west of a false summit en route, and approach the highest point from the northwest. The views from here are great. You can look north to the twelvers of the Kenosha Mountains and southeast to Bison Peak; Pikes Peak floats on the horizon beyond Bison.

## 6. Topaz Mountain    11,762 feet

See map 6, page 46

Topaz Mountain is 2.4 miles southeast of North Tarryall Peak and 2.9 miles south-southeast of Lost Pass. Topaz is a little lower than North Tarryall, but it is a larger massif. Two false summits flank the main 11,762-foot summit of Topaz. Point 11,687 is 0.4 mile northwest and Point 11,663 is 1.0 mile southeast. Point 11,663 is at the top of Hourglass Burn, a highly visible scar on both sides of the ridge. When viewing Topaz, it is difficult to identify the main summit. This problem is even greater when hiking on the peak. The main challenge Topaz presents is navigational. When you find it, the craggy summit offers you open views.

Point 11,687

Topaz Mountain
11,762

Hourglass Burn
11,663

*Topaz Mountain from Eagle Rock*

## Route
### 6.2 North Slopes
*From Lost Pass TH at 10,670 ft:*      *91 RP*   *7.3 mi*   *1,798 ft*   *Class 2*
*From 4WD parking at 10,750 ft:*     *47 RP*   *2.7 mi*   *1,028 ft*   *Class 2*

This is the easiest route on Topaz Mountain. It is a longer but easier hike than North Tarryall Peak's North Slopes Route. The north side of Topaz is home to many old logging roads. They can speed you on your way to the summit and remind you why these precious places need wilderness protection. Your footsteps will seem puny next to the logging scars.

Start at Lost Pass Trailhead, go 0.2 mile southeast on Lost Park Road and turn south (right) onto FS 446 (Topaz Road). Follow Topaz Road 1.1 miles southeast then west as it goes around a little ridge and crosses Beaver Creek at 10,650 feet. Continue 1.0 mile southeast then southwest on Topaz Road as it goes around another ridge and crosses Monkey Creek at 10,750 feet. When the road is dry, four-wheel-drive vehicles can reach this point. Continue 0.9 mile southeast, southwest and southeast on Topaz Road to its summit at 11,300 feet. Leave the road here and hike 100 yards south to the top of tiny Point 11,368, which is the westernmost of two Points 11,368. From this vantage, take a moment to observe the main summit of Topaz, which is south-southwest of you. When you have your bearings, hike 0.4 mile south-southwest to the highest point.

See
map 6,
page 46

## 6. North Tarryall and Topaz Combination

**6.3 No Tarry Top *Classic***

*From Lost Pass TH at 10,670 ft:*       *154 RP     8.4 mi     2,310 ft     Class 2*

This is the easiest way to ascend North Tarryall and Topaz together. Using the theory that it is best to gain elevation on the easiest terrain, ascend Topaz Mountain's North Slopes Route. From the summit of Topaz, hike 0.5 mile northwest and skirt Point 11,687 on its north side. Descend 0.9 mile northwest to the 11,030-foot saddle between Topaz and North Tarryall. Hike 0.6 mile northwest to a flat area and continue 0.4 mile northwest to treeline at 11,800 feet. Hike 0.1 mile southwest to North Tarryall's summit and descend North Tarryall's North Slopes Route.

See
map 7,
page 51

## 7. BISON GROUP

| | |
|---|---|
| **Bison Peak** | **12,431 feet** |
| **McCurdy Mountain** | **12,168 feet** |

We have arrived at the heartland of the Retirement Range. These are the range's two best peaks. Together, Bison and McCurdy are one large massif hidden in the center of the Retirement Range. The peaks are 12.5 miles south of Bailey on U.S. 285 and 13.5 miles north of Wilkerson Pass on U.S. 24, but you cannot see Bison and McCurdy from these highways. Your best views come from Tarryall Road immediately south of the peaks.

Both Bison and McCurdy have large areas above treeline, and you can roam at will on these summit plateaus. This is what the Retirement Range summits are famous for, and no peaks offer more summit freedom than Bison and McCurdy. Their summit plateaus are festooned with rock towers and formations. In your quest for Bison and McCurdy's highest points, you will see many of them.

### Maps

*Required: McCurdy Mountain, Farnum Peak*
*Optional: Topaz Mountain, Windy Peak*

### Trailheads

Ute Creek Trailhead

This trailhead is at 8,760 feet and provides access to Bison's southwest side and McCurdy's west side. You can approach this trailhead from the north or south.

For the northern approach, go to Jefferson on U.S. 285, turn onto Park County 77 (Tarryall Road) and measure from this point. Go southeast on Park County 77, stay straight (left) at 5.9 miles, stay straight (right) at

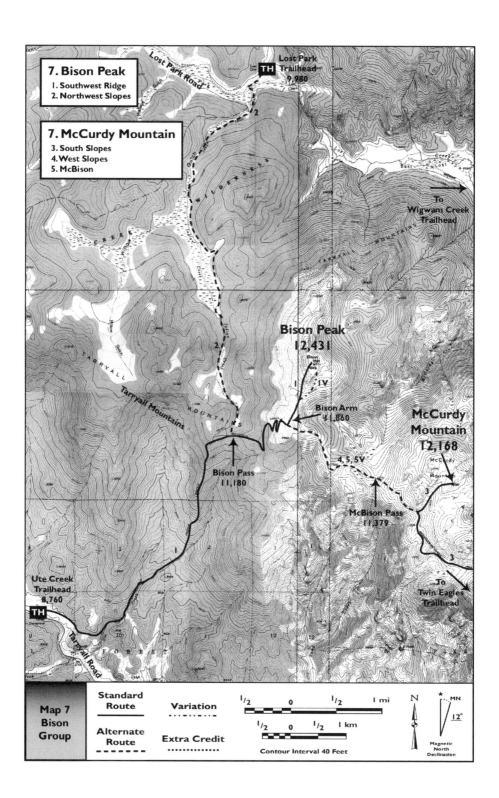

**7. Bison Peak**
1. Southwest Ridge
2. Northwest Slopes

**7. McCurdy Mountain**
3. South Slopes
4. West Slopes
5. McBison

Lost Park Road

Lost Park
Trailhead
9,980

TH

To
Wigwam Creek
Trailhead

WILDERNESS

CREEK

TARRYALL

Tarryall Mountains

MOUNTAINS

**Bison Peak**
**12,431**

1V

Bison Arm
11,860

**McCurdy**
**Mountain**
**12,168**

McCurdy
Mountain

3

Bison Pass
11,180

4, 5, 5V

McBison Pass
11,379

3

Ute Creek
Trailhead
8,760

TH

FOREST

Tarryall Road

To
Twin Eagles
Trailhead

3

| Map 7 Bison Group | Standard Route | Variation | ¹/₂   0   ¹/₂   1 mi | N | MN |
|---|---|---|---|---|---|
| | Alternate Route | Extra Credit | ¹/₂   0   ¹/₂   1 km |  | 12° |
| | | | Contour Interval 40 Feet | | Magnetic North Declination |

7.9 miles, stay straight (left) at 8.4 miles, pass Tarryall Reservoir, stay straight (left) at 16.9 miles and reach Ute Creek Trailhead at 20.2 miles.

For the southern approach, go to the spur road for Twin Eagles Trailhead on Park County 77 (see Twin Eagles Trailhead). From here, go 5.4 miles northeast on Park County 77 (Tarryall Road) to Ute Creek Trailhead. The signed trailhead and a parking area are on the road's north side. This trailhead is accessible in winter.

### Twin Eagles Trailhead

This trailhead is at 8,540 feet and provides access to McCurdy's south side and South Tarryall's north side. You can approach this trailhead from the north or south.

For the northern approach, go to Ute Creek Trailhead. From here, go 5.4 miles southeast on Park County 77 (Tarryall Road) to the signed turn for Twin Eagles Trailhead.

For the southern approach, go to the spur road 100 yards from Spruce Grove Trailhead on Park County 77 (see Spruce Grove Trailhead). From here, go 1.7 miles northeast on Park County 77 (Tarryall Road) to the signed turn for Twin Eagles Trailhead.

From the signed turn for Twin Eagles Trailhead, turn northeast (left) on a spur road and go 0.2 mile to the trailhead. There is a $3 fee to park at this trailhead. It is accessible in winter.

See
map 7,
page 51

# 7. Bison Peak      12,431 feet

Bison Peak is the highest peak in the Retirement Range. It carries this honor well and is justifiably popular. Bison is one of the Retirement Range's Big 4. If you cut Bison off at 12,000 feet, the resulting plateau would be 1.4 miles long! By that measure, Bison reigns supreme. Good trails reach high on the peak, and Bison is not as hard to ascend as other Retirement Range peaks. Because of the trails, you can ascend Bison without bushwhacking. That alone makes this peak special. If you have climbed all of Colorado's fourteeners but have never ascended Bison, make it your next outing.

### Routes
#### 7.1 Southwest Ridge *Classic*
*From Ute Creek TH at 8,760 ft:*      *157 RP    12.2 mi    3,671 ft    Class 1*

This is the most used route up Bison Peak. The hike is Class 1 all the way to the summit. The spectacular scenery on the summit plateau makes this one of our most recommended Retirement Range hikes. The low trailhead and southern aspect of the approach trail make this hike available much of the year. When higher peaks are buried in snow and you crave a little sunshine on your shoulders, try Bison. However, although the approach may

Bison Peak
12,431

Bison Arm
11,860

Bison Pass
11,180

53

*Bison Peak from the southwest*

warm you, the summit plateau we have been raving about can be a frozen, windswept place in winter. The authors ascended this route in April 1997. The approach was warm and the summit was frigid. This was Gerry's last Colorado training hike before climbing Gasherbrum II in the Karakorum.

Start at Ute Creek Trailhead, cross to Tarryall Creek's north side on a good bridge and hike 0.4 mile east-southeast on the excellent Ute Creek Trail. Do not worry; your lack of upward progress will soon be over. Hike 0.4 mile east-southeast then northeast through a little saddle and engage the ascent up Ute Creek. Hike 1.5 miles north-northeast on Ute Creek's west side to 9,600 feet and enter the Lost Creek Wilderness en route. Now for the big pull. Hike 1.5 miles north up a ridge west of Ute Creek to 11,240 feet. The trail is excellent and this ascent is where the sun can warm you. From 11,140 feet, hike 0.2 mile east to the junction with the Brookside-McCurdy Trail in 11,180-foot Bison Pass. From here, you can see Bison's upper massif to the northeast. You can also see Bison Arm to the east.

The Ute Creek Trail has done its job. It ends here in Bison Pass, and the Brookside-McCurdy Trail takes over. Hike 1.3 miles east on the Brookside-McCurdy Trail up six switchbacks to Bison Arm, a broad, 11,860-foot pass on Bison's south ridge. This is the highest point in the Lost Creek Wilderness that is reached by a trail. You are on top of the trail system!

There is more. The Brookside-McCurdy Trail has done its job, and you are now ready for your summit ride. Leave the trail and hike 0.4 mile north-

northeast to 12,000 feet. You will descend to and pass a spectacular, free-standing pinnacle en route. If you harbor any rock climbing urges, you can ponder an ascent route and, perhaps, vow to return for a future attempt. However, today we are ascending Bison.

Although 14,000 feet is magic elsewhere in Colorado, 12,000 feet is magic in the Retirement Range. Continue upward into the magic zone. Hike 0.2 mile north to 12,200 feet and stay west (left) of a rocky ridge. This ridge is festooned with Jurassic rocks. Hike 0.2 mile northeast and stay to the east (right) of the summit outcrop. Circle around to the summit's north side. Circle around some more and reach the summit from the west. The Retirement Range is yours.

**54**

### 7.1V Variation—Neffer's Way

From 12,000 feet hike around the east (right) side of the Jurassic ridge. Stay below the rocks. When you are north of the ridge, hike west up a slope and spot the summit rocks to the northwest. Hike northwest and rejoin the ascent route near the summit.

*The authors on Bison Arm (photo by Mike Butyn)*

### 7.2 Northwest Slopes *Classic*
*From Lost Park TH at 9,980 ft:*  147 RP  13.2 mi  2,531 ft  Class 1

This is a longer route up Bison Peak, and you are even deeper in the wilderness heartland. You start at a higher trailhead, and this reduces your elevation gain. However, while the Southwest Ridge Route is accessible for much of the year, this route is accessible only in summer and fall. Start at

*Bison's giant boulders*

Lost Park Trailhead and cross to the south side of the South Fork of Lost Creek. Hike 5.0 miles south on the Brookside-McCurdy Trail to Bison Pass. Join the Southwest Ridge Route there and follow it to the summit.

## 7. McCurdy Mountain    12,168 feet

Once, when flying into Denver from the southwest, we glanced out the window at dusk and saw a magnificent peak. Accustomed to always being

See map 7, page 51

See map 8, page 58

55

*McCurdy from Bison with Pikes in the background*

able to identify Colorado peaks from the air, we were confused. Jennifer exclaimed, "Wow! What is that?" Our minds quickly abandoned the airline's enclosed universe and we craned our necks for a better look. Pregnant seconds ticked by. After transitioning to a wilderness mind-set, Gerry said simply, "It's McCurdy." We gazed down on McCurdy's summit plateau with its myriad towers and rock outcrops gleaming in the late sun. Even at jet speed, it was a laconic passage. We tucked the incredible image deep in a memory pocket for future use.

Your authors agree that McCurdy is the finest peak in the Retirement Range. McCurdy is easily one of the Retirement Range's Big 4. Jennifer likes it so much that she has ascended it eight times. Once she ascended it on New Year's Day. McCurdy is a rock wonderland. Fantastic formations spread far beyond the summit plateau and even cover neighboring peaks. McCurdy, although lower than Bison, is larger than Bison. McCurdy does not have as much area above 12,000 feet as Bison, but if you truncated both peaks at 11,400 feet, McCurdy's plateau would be larger than Bison's.

McCurdy is 2.1 miles southeast of Bison. McCurdy is difficult to see from the north or east. In compensation, you have spectacular views of McCurdy from Tarryall Road near Twin Eagles and Spruce Grove Trailheads. Also, watch for McCurdy when you fly into Denver from the southwest.

*McCurdy from the southwest*

*The McCurdy Massif from the south-southeast*

## Routes

### 7.3 South Slopes *Classic*

*From Twin Eagles TH at 8,540 ft:*     *187 RP    14.4 mi    3,908 ft    Class 2*

This is the easiest route up mighty McCurdy Mountain, and it is a slightly harder hike than Bison's Southwest Ridge Route. The route follows the excellent Brookside-McCurdy Trail high on the mountain and, as with Bison, you do not have to bushwhack on this hike.

Start at Twin Eagles Trailhead, cross to the east side of Tarryall Creek on a good bridge and hike 0.3 mile northeast on the Brookside-McCurdy Trail. Cross an old road and continue 1.4 miles north on the Brookside-McCurdy Trail as it skirts private property to a trail junction with the Hankins Pass Trail at 8,920 feet. During this approach, you will be treated to views of McCurdy draped in rocks to the north.

Continue 1.0 mile north on the Brookside-McCurdy Trail up some short switchbacks to the Lost Creek Wilderness boundary at 9,480 feet. Your

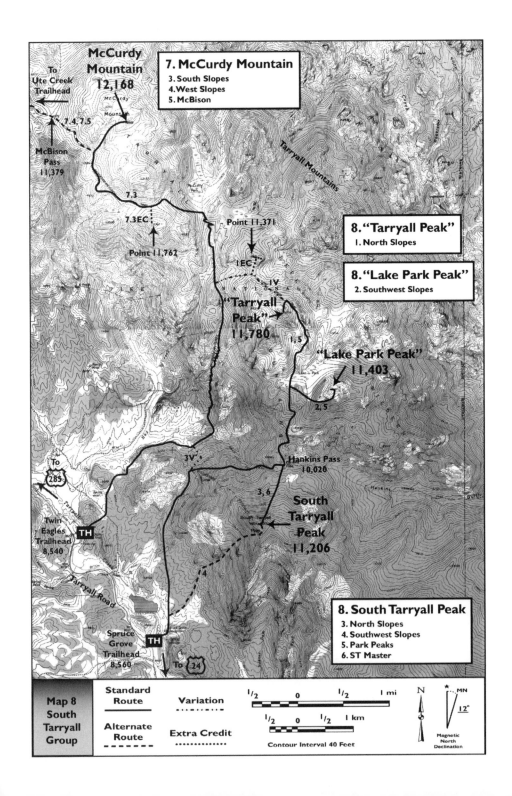

McCurdy
Mountain
12,168

To
Ute Creek
Trailhead

7.4,7.5

McBison
Pass
11,379

7.3

7.3EC

Point 11,762

Point 11,371

1EC

1V

"Tarryall
Peak"
11,780

1,5

"Lake Park Peak"
11,403

2,5

Tarryall Mountains

3V

Hankins Pass
10,020

3,6

South
Tarryall
Peak
11,206

To
285

Twin
Eagles
Trailhead
8,540

TH

Tarryall Road

4

Spruce
Grove
Trailhead
8,560

TH

To 24

### 7. McCurdy Mountain
3. South Slopes
4. West Slopes
5. McBison

### 8. "Tarryall Peak"
1. North Slopes

### 8. "Lake Park Peak"
2. Southwest Slopes

### 8. South Tarryall Peak
3. North Slopes
4. Southwest Slopes
5. Park Peaks
6. ST Master

Map 8
South
Tarryall
Group

Standard
Route

Variation

Alternate
Route

Extra Credit

1/2    0    1/2    1 mi

1/2    0    1/2    1 km

Contour Interval 40 Feet

N

MN

12°

Magnetic
North
Declination

Point 12,157    Point 11,762

*Approaching McCurdy on the Brookside-McCurdy Trail*

ascent has just begun. Continue 1.2 miles north up a series of tight switch-backs and beyond to a trail junction with the Lake Park Trail in a small sad-dle at 10,740 feet. Midway through the switchbacks, look for an arch in the rocks to the west. From the saddle, stay on the Brookside-McCurdy Trail and descend 0.2 mile north to a meadow at 10,600 feet. It is on this north-facing slope that you will first find snow during the shoulder seasons. From the meadow, hike 0.8 mile north to a trail junction with the McCurdy Park Trail in the 10,900-foot saddle between McCurdy Mountain and the wild Point 11,460 to the east. From this saddle, you can look down on McCurdy Park to the north.

From the 10,900-foot saddle, stay on the Brookside-McCurdy Trail and hike 0.7 mile west to an 11,420-foot saddle between McCurdy to the north and Point 11,762 to the south. This saddle is full of highly eroded bristlecone pines, and this is a stark but beautiful area. Resist any temptation to leave the trail and head for McCurdy just yet. The slopes above this saddle are rough, and it is still a long way to the summit. This is the mighty McCurdy of lore. Continue 0.6 mile west on the trail to a shoulder at 11,520 feet, cross the shoulder and hike 0.5 mile north to 11,540 feet. Now is the time to head for the heights.

When the trail turns west, leave it and hike 0.4 mile northeast up a broad gully to 12,000 feet (Class 2). Hike 0.1 mile east to McCurdy's summit rocks, which resist easy passage on three sides. Hike to the northwest end of the summit rocks, climb 50 feet up a north-facing ramp and scamper 15 feet east to the highest point (Class 2). McCurdy has a 12,164-foot northwestern summit. The 12,168-foot southeastern summit described here is McCurdy's summit. Do not confuse these two summits. Enjoy your summit stay and wave at any jets passing overhead. You never know who might be watching and wishing they were on McCurdy instead of in an airplane. Perhaps they can catch your wave.

### 7.3EC Extra Credit—Point 11,762

| | | | | |
|---|---|---|---|---|
| *From 11,420 ft:* | *16 RP* | *0.4 mi* | *342 ft* | *Class 2* |
| *With McCurdy:* | *204 RP* | *14.8 mi* | *4,250 ft* | *Class 2* |

If McCurdy is not enough for you, hike 0.2 mile south from the 11,420-foot saddle to Point 11,762. This peak is a ranked elevener, the fifth-highest

*Arch near the Brookside-McCurdy Trail*

peak in the Tarryall Mountains; even better, it gives you an unusual perspective on McCurdy.

### 7.4 West Slopes *Classic*
*From Ute Creek TH at 8,760 ft:*      *202 RP   15.4 mi   4,329 ft   Class 2*

This is an aesthetically rewarding route up McCurdy Mountain. Most of the hike is on excellent trails. Only the summit ride is Class 2. You have to regain some elevation on the return, and that extra gain keeps this from being McCurdy's easiest route.

Start at Ute Creek Trailhead and follow Bison's Southwest Ridge Route to Bison Arm at 11,860 feet. Continue 1.3 miles east on the Brookside-McCurdy Trail and descend to 11,379-foot McBison Pass between Bison and McCurdy. This is one of the most privileged positions in the Lost Creek

*Treeline on McCurdy*

Wilderness. You can look northwest to Bison, and McCurdy's mass is east of you. From McBison Pass, hike 0.6 mile east-southeast on the Brookside-McCurdy Trail as it ascends to 11,580 feet, then gently descends to 11,540 feet. During this stretch, watch the terrain north of the trail. You are looking for the easternmost of three broad gully systems.

When the trail turns south, leave it and begin your summit ride. Hike 0.4 mile northeast up the broad gully to 12,000 feet (Class 2). Hike 0.1 mile east to McCurdy's summit rocks, which resist easy passage on three sides. Hike to the northwest end of the summit rocks, climb 50 feet up a north-facing ramp and scamper 15 feet east to the highest point (Class 2). Continue the wave.

**62**

## 7. Bison and McCurdy Combination

**7.5 McBison *Classic***

See map 7, page 51

See map 8, page 58

*From Ute Creek TH at 8,760 ft:        238 RP   15.1 mi    5,341 ft   Class 2*

This is the easiest way to ascend Bison and McCurdy together without a vehicle shuttle. Start at Ute Creek Trailhead and ascend Bison's Southwest Ridge Route. From Bison's summit, return to the Brookside-McCurdy Trail on Bison Arm at 11,860 feet. Continue on the upper part of McCurdy's West Slopes Route. Descend McCurdy's West Slopes Route.

*Bison and McCurdy from Badger Mountain*

### 7.5V Variation
*Descent to Twin Eagles TH at 8,540 ft:241 RP   16.5 mi   4,820 ft   Class 2*

With a vehicle shuttle between Twin Eagles and Ute Creek Trailheads, you can descend McCurdy's South Slopes Route and enjoy a grand Tour de Bison and McCurdy. By descending McCurdy's South Slopes Route, you eliminate the need to reascend Bison Arm on the return, but you increase the mileage. At the end of the day, your total effort expenditure is nearly the same.

# 8. SOUTH TARRYALL GROUP

| | |
|---|---|
| **"Tarryall Peak"** | **11,780 feet** |
| **"Lake Park Peak"** | **11,403 feet** |
| **South Tarryall Peak** | **11,206 feet** |

63

See map 8, page 58

These three eleveners anchor the southeast end of the Tarryall Range. "Tarryall Peak" and "Lake Park Peak" command the rough country around Lake Park, which is 3.5 miles southeast of McCurdy Mountain. South Tarryall Peak is 0.7 mile south-southwest of Hankins Pass, which is 1.0 mile south of Lake Park. You can see these peaks from the Tarryall Road to the west. The peak's flanks are festooned with rock towers, slabs and alcoves. Good trails reach Lake Park and Hankins Pass, so the approach to these peaks is easy. The summits, however, are wild and rocky. A visit to any of these summits will offer you the essence of the Lost Creek Wilderness.

## Maps
*Required: McCurdy Mountain*
*Optional: Tarryall*

## Trailhead
### Spruce Grove Trailhead
This trailhead is at 8,560 feet and provides access to South Tarryall's north and south sides. You can approach this trailhead from the north or the south.

For the northern approach, go to the signed turn for Twin Eagles Trailhead on Park County 77 (see Twin Eagles Trailhead). From here, go 1.7 miles southeast on Park County 77 (Tarryall Road) to the signed turn for Spruce Grove Campground.

For the southern approach, go to Lake George on U.S. 24. Lake George is 13.5 miles west of Divide and 10.6 miles east of Wilkerson Pass. From Lake George, go 1.1 miles northwest on U.S. 24, turn north (right) onto Park County 77 (Tarryall Road) and measure from this point. Go north-

northeast on Park County 77, pass Happy Meadows Campground at 1.3 miles, go straight (right) at 11.6 miles and reach the signed turn for Spruce Grove Campground at 13.2 miles.

From the signed turn for Spruce Grove Campground, turn northeast onto a spur road, go 100 yards north and park in a parking area at the top of a hill overlooking Spruce Grove Campground. There is a good view of South Tarryall Peak and McCurdy Mountain from here. Day hikers cannot park in the campground. To start your hike, go 100 yards northeast, take the first right into the campground, go down and find the hiking trailhead 50 feet east of the restrooms. This trailhead is accessible in winter.

## 8. "Tarryall Peak"    11,780 feet

"Tarryall Peak" is 2.8 miles southeast of McCurdy Mountain. The peak does not have an official name but is the summit of the southeast end of the Tarryall Range. It is the fourth-highest peak in the Tarryalls. The peak's specified altitude of 11,758 feet is lower than the highest contour, and we use the higher, interpolated altitude of 11,780 feet. Although close to a good trail, the summit of "Tarryall Peak" is rocky, wild and seldom visited. The summit provides intimate views of McCurdy Mountain and Lost Creek's twisted canyons to the north. "Tarryall Peak" is a splendid encore to Bison and McCurdy's excitement.

### Route
#### 8.1 North Slopes *Classic*
*From Spruce Grove TH at 8,560 ft:*    *135 RP    11.2 mi    3,420 ft    Class 2+*

This is the easiest route on "Tarryall Peak," and it is an excellent outing for newcomers to the Retirement Range. It follows good trails most of the way. The short summit scamper will excite and remove you from civilization.

Start at Spruce Grove Trailhead, go 100 yards northeast, take the first right into Spruce Grove Campground, go down and find the hiking trailhead 50 feet east of the restrooms. Cross to Tarryall Creek's east side on a good bridge and hike 2.0 miles north on the Lizard Rock Trail to a trail junction with the Hankins Pass Trail in a 9,300-foot saddle that is 1.0 mile northwest of South Tarryall Peak. Turn east (right), enter the Lost Creek Wilderness and hike 1.1 miles east on the Hankins Pass Trail to a marked trail junction in 10,020-foot Hankins Pass.

In Hankins Pass, turn north (left) on the Lake Park Trail and hike 1.1 miles north past several interesting rock outcrops to a 10,900-foot saddle above the southwest end of Lake Park. The trail's approach to the 10,900-foot saddle is incorrectly marked on both the McCurdy Mountain Quadrangle and the Trails Illustrated Map number 105. The trail is west of

*"Tarryall Peak"*

the maps' markings. Descend slightly and hike 0.2 mile north across Lake Park's higher, west end. From here, you can see "Tarryall Peak" 0.8 mile to the north. It looks rocky and imposing. Do not confuse Point 11,695 with 11,780-foot "Tarryall Peak." Point 11,695 is 0.3 mile south-southwest of "Tarryall Peak" and is even more imposing.

From the northwest corner of Lake Park, hike 1.0 mile north, west, then north again to the trail's summit in a small saddle at 11,540 feet. This scenic section of trail passes through several intimate glens. Leave the trail in the 11,540-foot saddle and hike 180 yards southwest through open trees (Class 2). Snow can persist on this slope into June. As you approach the summit rocks, get into and ascend a little rock gully (Class 2+). As you approach the summit ridge, hike 20 yards southeast to the highest point (Class 2+). Most of the grand views will appear in the last few steps.

### 8.1 V Variation
*From Spruce Grove TH at 8,560 ft:*  150 RP  12.0 mi  4,100 ft  Class 2+

You can use the Brookside-McCurdy Trail to approach "Tarryall Peak." Start at Spruce Grove Trailhead and follow the North Slopes Route 2.1 miles north on the Lizard Rock Trail to the junction with the Hankins Pass Trail at 9,300 feet. Descend 0.5 mile north on the beginning of the Hankins Pass Trail to the Brookside-McCurdy Trail at 8,920 feet. Hike 1.0 mile north on the Brookside-McCurdy Trail up some short switchbacks to the Lost Creek Wilderness boundary at 9,480 feet. Continue 1.2 miles north up a series of

*A Tarryall morning*

tight switchbacks and beyond to a trail junction with the Lake Park Trail in a small saddle at 10,740 feet. Midway through the switchbacks, look for an arch in the rocks to the west.

Leave the Brookside-McCurdy Trail in the small saddle at 10,740 feet. Turn east (right) and hike 0.5 mile east up the Lake Park Trail to an 11,100-foot saddle between Point 11,371 and "Tarryall Peak." Continue 0.6 mile southeast on the Lake Park Trail to its summit in the small, 11,540-foot saddle. Rejoin the North Slopes Route there for the summit scamper. Ascending this variation and descending the North Slopes Route makes a terrific Tour de Tarryall.

### 8.1EC Extra Credit—Point 11,371

For extra excitement and views when doing the 8.1V Variation, leave the Lake Park Trail in the 11,100-foot saddle. Hike 0.2 mile north to the 11,260-foot saddle between the two summits of Point 11,371. For the easiest tour, hike 100 yards east up some rough boulders to the eastern summit (Class 2). This summit is slightly lower but easier to reach than the western summit. For maximum excitement, hike 100 yards west from the 11,260-foot saddle and climb the higher, western summit. The highest point is difficult to discern from below. It is the southernmost choice. Climb ramps and a gully to reach the summit ridge south of the summit (Class 3). Climb north on or near the ridge to the highest point (Class 4). This unique rock summit offers an uninterrupted view of McCurdy.

# 8. "Lake Park Peak"   11,403 feet

*See map 8, page 58*

"Lake Park Peak" is 1.0 mile south-southeast of "Tarryall Peak," 0.3 mile south-southeast of Lake Park and 1.0 mile north-northeast of Hankins Pass. The peak's steep north face forms the south wall of Lake Park. The peak has two summits; the western summit is slightly higher. The Lake Park Trail provides an easy approach, but the summit rocks are rugged. From the summit, you have exceptional views to the north of Point 11,695, "Tarryall Peak" and McCurdy Mountain.

## Route

### 8.2 Southwest Slopes

*From Spruce Grove TH at 8,560 ft:*    *125 RP    10.0 mi    3,043 ft    Class 2+*

This is the easiest route on "Lake Park Peak." Although lower than "Tarryall Peak," "Lake Park Peak" has a longer, rougher summit scamper. Start at Spruce Grove Trailhead and follow the North Slopes Route on "Tarryall Peak" to the 10,900-foot saddle above the southwest end of Lake Park. Leave the trail here and hike 0.4 mile east-southeast to reach the southwest ridge of "Lake Park Peak" at 11,100 feet. Cross to the ridge's south side, descend slightly and climb 0.2 mile east across rough boulders (Class 2+). Avoid any temptation to cut up toward the summit too soon. Cross a little south ridge. When you can see the eastern summit, turn north (left) and

*"Lake Park Peak" from Lake Park*

scamper 0.1 mile north to the top of the western summit (Class 2+). This is the mountain's highpoint. From here, you can peer down on Lake Park.

See map 8, page 58

# 8. South Tarryall Peak 11,206 feet

South Tarryall Peak is 4.7 miles south-southeast of McCurdy Mountain and 0.7 mile south-southwest of Hankins Pass. Unlike its higher neighbors around Lake Park, South Tarryall Peak is named, and the peak is the monarch of the southern Tarryall Mountains. South Tarryall is the southern-most elevener in the Tarryall Mountains and, by that measure, anchors the southern end of this rich range. South Tarryall is only 1.8 miles northeast of Spruce Grove Trailhead on Tarryall Road, and you can easily see the peak from there. South Tarryall is just high enough to have an open summit with views. The peak is on the edge of the Lost Creek Wilderness.

## Routes

### 8.3 North Slopes *Classic*
*From Spruce Grove TH at 8,540 ft:*    *114 RP    8.2 mi    2,766 ft    Class 2*

This is the easiest route on South Tarryall. It follows good trails to Hankins Pass on the peak's north side, then requires a modest bushwhack to the summit. Start at Spruce Grove Trailhead, go 100 yards northeast, take the first right into Spruce Grove Campground, go down and find the hiking trailhead 50 feet east of the restrooms. Cross to Tarryall Creek's east side on a good bridge and hike 2.0 miles north on the Lizard Rock Trail to a trail junction with the Hankins Pass Trail in a 9,300-foot saddle that is 1.0 mile northwest of South Tarryall Peak. Turn east (right), enter the Lost Creek Wilderness and hike 1.1 miles east on the Hankins Pass Trail to a trail junction in 10,020-foot Hankins Pass. Leave the trail and bushwhack 0.75 mile southwest up a wooded slope to the summit. From here, you have a stunning view of McCurdy and Bison.

### 8.3V Variation
*From Twin Eagles TH at 8,540 ft:*    *114 RP    8.3 mi    2,666 ft    Class 2*

This variation requires the same effort as the North Slopes Route. Start at Twin Eagles Trailhead. Follow the Brookside-McCurdy Trail 1.7 miles north to a trail junction with the Hankins Pass Trail. Leave the Brookside-McCurdy Trail, turn south (right) onto the Hankins Pass Trail and follow it 0.5 mile south to a trail junction with the Lizard Rock Trail in a 9,300-foot saddle. Join the North Slopes Route here and follow it to the summit.

### 8.4 Southwest Slopes
*From Spruce Grove TH at 8,560 ft:*    *103 RP    2.9 mi    2,766 ft    Class 2*

This is the shortest route on South Tarryall Peak. However, this stiff bushwhack is not the easiest route on South Tarryall; it is the proverbial shortcut. Study the peak before you start. Once you are in the trees, route finding becomes more difficult. Take care to follow the route described here. If you stray to the left or right, you will find rough terrain complete with mazes of car-sized boulders laced with deadfall. Add a little snow and you have a formula for a tough day.

Start your hike at the Spruce Grove Trailhead. From the bridge over Tarryall Creek, hike 0.2 mile north on the Lizard Rock Trail. You can see the peak from here above open meadows. Your route from here to the summit is very nearly a straight line. Leave the trail and hike 0.5 mile northeast directly toward the summit to 8,800 feet. Between you and the summit is a gully that is your key to a less than wretched passage. Massive cliffs flank the gully's north side, and two smaller buttresses guard the gully's south side. Hike another 0.6 mile northeast up this gully to 9,700 feet. The crux is over. Hike 0.5 mile northeast to the summit, staying north of any significant rock formations that appear in your path. Ascending the Southwest Slopes Route and descending the North Slopes Route makes a smart Tour de South Tarryall.

# 8. South Tarryall Group Combinations
## 8.5 Park Peaks
*From Spruce Grove TH at 8,560 ft:    171 RP    12.6 mi    4,003 ft  Class 2+*

*See map 8, page 58*

This is the easiest way to ascend "Tarryall Peak" and "Lake Park Peak" together. After investing in the hike to Lake Park, it makes sense to climb

*South Tarryall Peak from Spruce Grove Trailhead*

both peaks. Start at the Spruce Grove Trailhead and ascend the North Slopes Route on "Tarryall Peak." Return to the 10,900-foot saddle above the southwest end of Lake Park. Continue up the Southwest Slopes Route to the summit of "Lake Park Peak" and descend its Southwest Slopes Route.

### 8.6 ST Master

*From Spruce Grove TH at 8,560 ft:     226 RP    14.1 mi    5,189 ft   Class 2+*

For a clean South Tarryall sweep, this tour adds South Tarryall Peak to the Park Peaks tour. Follow the Park Peaks tour to the summits of "Tarryall Peak" and "Lake Park Peak." Return to Hankins Pass. Ascend the top part of the North Slopes Route of South Tarryall Peak and descend that peak's North Slopes Route.

*There is a pleasure in the pathless woods,*
*There is a rapture on the lonely shore,*
*There is society, where none intrudes,*
*By the deep Sea, and music in its roar:*
*O love not Man the less, but Nature more,*
*From these our interviews, in which I steal*
*For all I may be, or have been before,*
*To mingle with the Universe, and feel*
*What I can ne'er express,*
*Yet can not all conceal.*

—Lord Byron

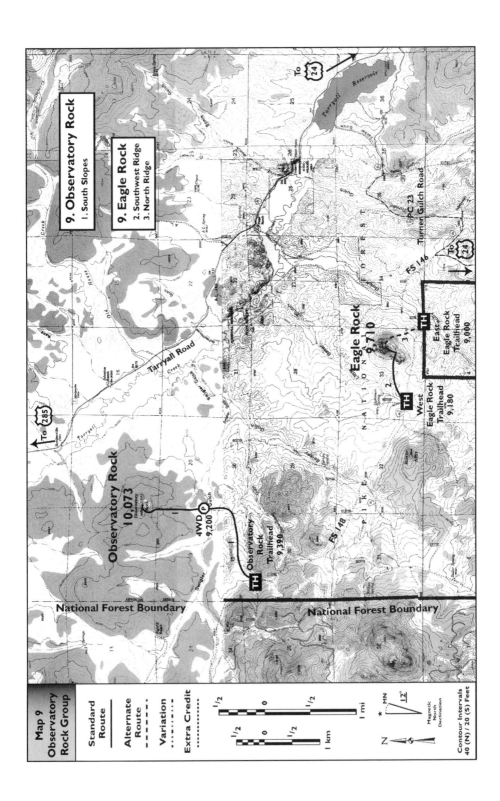

Map 9
Observatory
Rock Group

9. Observatory Rock
1. South Slopes

9. Eagle Rock
2. Southwest Ridge
3. North Ridge

Standard Route
Alternate Route
Variation
Extra Credit

1/2   0   1/2   1 mi
1/2   0   1/2   1 km

N    ★ MN
          12°
     Magnetic
     North
     Declination

Contour Intervals
40 (N) / 20 (S) Feet

Observatory Rock
10,073

National Forest Boundary

Tarryall Road

To 285

Tarryall Creek

4WD
9,200

Observatory Rock Trailhead
9,390

FS 148

National Forest Boundary

Eagle Rock
9,710

West Eagle Rock Trailhead
9,180

East Eagle Rock Trailhead
9,000

NATIONAL FOREST

PIKE

FS 146

Turner Gulch Road
PC 23

To 24

To 24

Tarryall Reservoir

*chapter four*

# Puma Hills

## Introduction

The Puma Hills are south of the Tarryall Road, east of U.S. 285 south of
Jefferson, and mostly north of U.S. 24 near Wilkerson Pass. More precisely,
the Puma Hills are bounded by Tarryall Creek on the north, the South Platte
River on the east and south, the Middle Fork of the South Platte River on
the southwest and U.S. 285 between the Middle Fork of the South Platte
and Tarryall Creek on the northwest.

In this chapter, we describe every named or ranked peak over 11,000 feet
in the Puma Hills. All of these summits are in the Pike National Forest, but
none of them are in the Lost Creek Wilderness. We describe the summits
from northwest to southeast.

Lower than their higher neighbors to the north, the Puma Hills are
rolling and pastoral. Many of their summits are tree covered and do not provide good views. The hikes to them are nice, however, and a fair number of
the summits do have fine views. In particular, the view from Observatory
Rock is one of the best in the Retirement Range. With or without views, you
can spend many pleasant days roaming over these summits. A list of all the
summits in the Puma Hills is in the Appendix.

## 9. OBSERVATORY ROCK GROUP

| | |
|---|---|
| **Observatory Rock** | **10,073 feet** |
| **Eagle Rock** | **9,710 feet** |

See
map 9,
page 72

The summits of these two rocks provide outstanding views. From their iso-
lated, rocky summits, you can survey most of the Tarryall Range and Puma
Hills. To the west, you can see the high peaks of the Mosquito Range.
Looking south, you can even see the northern Sangre de Cristo Range.

## Maps
*Required: Observatory Rock, Eagle Rock*
*Optional: Farnum Peak*

## Trailheads
### Observatory Rock Trailhead
This trailhead is at 9,390 feet and provides access to Observatory Rock's south side. Go to the small town of Jefferson on U.S. 285, 4.2 miles southwest of the summit of Kenosha Pass and 16.7 miles northeast of the U.S. 285–Colorado 9 junction south of Fairplay. Find the U.S. 285–Park County 77 junction in the center of Jefferson and measure from this point. Go southeast on Park County 77, stay straight (left) at 5.9 miles, stay straight (right) at 7.9 miles and turn south (right) onto Stagestop Road at 8.4 miles. Go south on Stagestop Road and turn east (left) onto Long Bow Drive at 11.9 miles. Go east then south on Long Bow Drive and turn east (left) onto FS 148 at 13.1 miles. Enter the Pike National Forest and go south then east on FS 148 to a sharp, south turn in the road at 13.4 miles. Park on the road's east side; this is the trailhead. This trailhead is often accessible in winter. Observatory Rock, which has not been visible during your approach to the trailhead, is visible 1.4 miles northeast of the trailhead.

Four-wheel-drive vehicles can get closer to Observatory Rock. Measuring from the trailhead, go south on FS 148, turn east (left) onto Observatory Rock Road at 0.6 mile, go northeast and turn west (left) at 2.7 miles. Go west up Swigler Gulch and park in an open area at 9,200 feet directly south of Observatory Rock at 3.2 miles. The rock is 0.7 mile north of this point.

### East Eagle Rock Trailhead
This trailhead is at 9,000 feet and provides access to Eagle Rock's east side. From Jefferson on U.S. 285, turn onto Park County 77 and measure from this point. Go southeast on Park County 77, stay straight (left) at 5.9 miles, stay straight (right) at 7.9 miles, stay straight (left) at 8.4 miles, pass Tarryall Reservoir and turn south onto Park County 23 at 16.9 miles. Park County 23 (Turner Gulch Road) goes south from here to U.S. 24. Go south then east on Turner Gulch Road, pass a view of Observatory and Eagle Rocks at 17.9 miles, go west (right) at 18.5 miles, go west (right) at 19.9 miles and turn northwest (right) onto FS 146 at 20.3 miles. Go northwest then west on FS 146, descend into Ruby Gulch, turn south-southwest (left) at 21.1 miles, turn west (right) at 21.4 miles, cross to the west side of a cattle guard and park. This is the trailhead. You can see Eagle Rock northwest of here.

### West Eagle Rock Trailhead

This trailhead is at 9,180 feet and provides access to Eagle Rock's west side. From East Eagle Rock Trailhead, go 0.55 mile west on FS 146 and park. This is the trailhead. Four-wheel-drive vehicles can go to Observatory Rock Trailhead from here. To do it, continue west on FS 146, go straight (right) onto FS 148 at 1.4 miles, go straight (left) at 1.6 miles, continue northwest then north and reach Observatory Rock Trailhead at 3.2 miles. This connection makes it easy to ascend Eagle Rock and Observatory Rock on the same day.

## 9. Observatory Rock    10,073 feet

Observatory Rock is 4.7 miles northwest of the Tarryall Reservoir. The rock sits atop an isolated uplift in the rolling country west of the main Puma Hills. The rock is only 1.1 miles southwest of the Tarryall Reservoir Road at one point, but private property and a difficult ford of Tarryall Creek preclude hiking from there. The rock is best seen from the south, which is the side that does have good access. Observatory Rock is well named. From the summit, you can see forever. All you have to do is look beyond the horizon. Even if you cannot manage that, the horizon alone is wonderful.

75

See map 9, page 72

*Observatory Rock from the south*

*Looking down Observatory Rock's summit gully*

## Route
### 9.1 South Slopes *Classic*
*From Observatory Rock TH at 9,390 ft: 37 RP    3.4 mi   1,063 ft Class 2+*
*From 4WD parking at 9,200 ft:        25 RP    1.4 mi    873 ft Class 2+*

This is a short hike and scamper to an open, rock summit. Start at Observatory Rock Trailhead and hike 0.7 mile east down an open meadow and cross to the north side of a fence en route. When you are south of Observatory Rock, hike 0.3 mile north over a slight rise, cross Swigler Gulch and reach the road just north of Swigler Gulch. This is the four-wheel-drive parking spot. Hike 0.5 mile north up a small gulch to 9,440 feet. Hike up the steepening slope above to a point 150 yards west of the summit and hike east to the summit tower. Find a gully in the middle of the tower's west face with a large, twisted tree at the bottom of it. This is the route. Scamper 100 feet up this Class 2+ gully to the summit. The hardest moves are on rock near the top.

Observe carefully from the summit. This is a great place to review the Retirement Range. You can see the highest peak in the Platte River Mountains, the Kenosha Mountains, the Tarryall Mountains and the Puma Hills. You might even see a puma.

# 9. Eagle Rock      9,710 feet

Eagle Rock is 3.2 miles southeast of Observatory Rock and 2.5 miles west-southwest of the Tarryall Reservoir. Like Observatory Rock, Eagle Rock is an isolated uplift with a dramatic rock summit. It is easier to ascend than Observatory Rock and offers a choice of routes. If you were an eagle, you could approach your summit from above. Alas, you must ascend Eagle Rock from below, but it is not hard.

77

See map 9, page 72

## Routes
### 9.2 Southwest Ridge
*From West Eagle Rock TH at 9,180 ft:     16 RP     0.9 mi      530 ft  Class 2*

For minimalists, this is it. This is the easiest route on Eagle Rock and the shortest route in this book. Start at West Eagle Rock Trailhead and hike 0.25 mile north on an old road to 9,280 feet below Eagle Rock's west side. This road is closed to vehicles. One hundred yards before the road goes into

*Eagle Rock from the southeast*

the trees and ends, leave it and hike 0.1 mile through the trees to 9,420 feet on Eagle Rock's southwest ridge. Turn north (left) and climb 0.1 mile northeast to the summit via a scruffy gully in the middle of Eagle Rock's southwest ridge.

### 9.3 North Ridge *Classic*
*From East Eagle Rock TH at 9,000 ft:    21 RP     1.2 mi      710 ft Class 2+*

This route is slightly harder and more adventurous than Eagle Rock's Southwest Ridge Route, but it is a little easier than Observatory Rock's South Slopes Route. Start at East Eagle Rock Trailhead and hike 0.35 mile north-northwest to 9,150 feet below Eagle Rock's east side. Hike 0.2 mile north-

*The hidden ramp on Eagle Rock*

west up a rough slope to the 9,650-foot saddle between Eagle Rock's main and north summits. From the saddle, the 9,677-foot north summit is only 100 feet north and is worth a visit. This vantage gives you a chance to preview the rest of the route on the main summit. You can see only part of it. Return to the saddle.

From the saddle, hike 120 feet north on a ledge on the west side of the main summit's north ridge. When the route looks improbable, peer south around a corner and behold a hidden ramp leading northeast. Climb the ramp to the crest of the main summit's north ridge (Class 2). Scamper 50 feet south up the ridge to a false summit (Class 2+). Scamper 40 feet south across an exposed notch to Eagle Rock's highest point (Class 2+). Ascending the North Ridge Route and descending the Southwest Ridge Route makes a smart Tour de Eagle Rock.

## 10. Puma Peak Group

| | | |
|---|---|---|
| "Puma Peak" | 11,570 feet | |
| "Little Puma" | 11,449 feet | |
| Farnum Peak | 11,377 feet | |
| "Burntop" | 11,085 feet | |

See map 10, page 80

This is the Puma Hills' highest massif, and "Puma Peak," "Little Puma" and Farnum Peak are the Puma Hills' three highest peaks. The massif is 4.5 miles south-southeast of Tarryall Reservoir. Unlike the open, rock summits of Observatory and Eagle Rocks, these summits are tree covered. The route up the main massif is on a road through thick trees on a north-facing slope. This massif gives you a chance to examine the forest and reflect on the small things beneath your feet. These are some of the easiest hikes in this book.

### Maps

*Required: Farnum Peak*
*Optional: Eagle Rock*

### Trailhead

#### Packer Gulch Trailhead

This trailhead is at 9,700 feet and provides access to the north sides of "Puma Peak" and "Little Puma," and Farnum Peak's west ridge. From Jefferson on U.S. 285, turn onto Park County 77 (Tarryall Road) and measure from this point. Go southeast on Park County 77, stay straight (left) at 5.9 miles, stay straight (right) at 7.9 miles, stay straight (left) at 8.4 miles, pass Tarryall Reservoir and turn south onto Park County 23 (Turner Gulch Road) at 16.9 miles. Go south then east on Turner Gulch Road and turn south (left) onto FS 144 (Packer Gulch Road) at 18.5 miles. Go south on

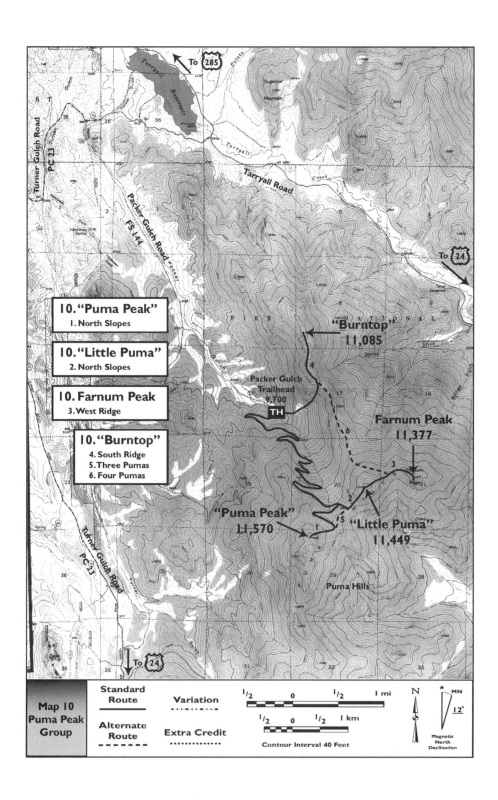

Map 10
Puma Peak
Group

*The Puma Peak Group from the northwest*

Packer Gulch Road, turn south-southeast (left) at 18.8 miles, go straight (left) at 20.2 miles, turn south-southeast (left) at 21.0 miles and reach the trailhead at 22.5 miles. Park just before the road turns west, crosses Packer Creek and enters the trees. Four-wheel-drive vehicles can go farther. The Forest Service road closure gate is 100 yards beyond the first switchback.

# 10. "Puma Peak"   11,570 feet

See map 10, page 80

"Puma Peak" is the highest peak in the Puma Hills, and it reflects the Puma Hills' relaxed nature. Your hike to the highest point will stretch your legs and reward you with time away from the city.

## Route

### 10.1 North Slopes *Classic*

*From Packer Gulch TH at 9,700 ft:*    83 RP    6.6 mi    1,870 ft    Class 2

This is the easiest route up "Puma Peak." Start at Packer Gulch Trailhead and hike 3.0 miles up the road (FS 144) past 11 switchbacks to a small saddle at 11,060 feet on the northeast ridge of "Puma Peak." This is the end of the road. Hike 0.3 mile west-southwest through open trees to the Puma Hills' highest point.

The Farnum Peak Quadrangle shows this point as 11,550 feet and an elevation of 11,570 feet 0.25 mile southwest. For once, the map is wrong. We made careful hand-level measurements and determined that the summit with a given altitude of 11,550 feet is higher than the summit with a given altitude of 11,570 feet. Until the USGS can correct this error, we give "Puma Peak" the altitude of 11,570 feet. The good news is that you do not have to hike the last 0.25 mile.

See map 10, page 80

## 10. "Little Puma"    11,449 feet

"Little Puma" is 0.8 miles northeast of "Puma Peak" and 0.6 mile west of Farnum Peak. Hiding between these important peaks, "Little Puma" is splendid in its obscurity. "Little Puma" is the second-highest peak in the Puma Hills.

82

**Route**

### 10.2 North Slopes

*From Packer Gulch TH at 9,700 ft:*    79 RP    5.4 mi    1,749 ft    Class 2

This is the easiest route up "Little Puma." It is an easier hike than "Puma Peak." Start at Packer Gulch Trailhead and hike 2.3 miles up the road (FS 144) to the tenth switchback at 10,820 feet. Leave the road and hike 0.1 mile southeast to the 10,954-foot saddle between "Puma Peak" and "Little Puma." Hike 0.3 mile northeast to the summit of "Little Puma." The summit is tree covered and does not offer great views, but at least there is no question about where the summit is.

See map 10, page 80

## 10. Farnum Peak    11,377 feet

Farnum Peak is 0.6 mile east of "Little Puma." Farnum Peak is the third-highest peak in the Puma Hills, but it does not rank. Unlike its higher neighbors, Farnum has an official name, probably because you can see this peak from the Tarryall Road south of the Tarryall Reservoir.

**Route**

### 10.3 West Ridge

*From Packer Gulch TH at 9,700 ft:*    105 RP    6.6 mi    2,375 ft    Class 2

This is the easiest route up Farnum Peak, and it will extend your "Little Puma" hike. Start at Packer Gulch Trailhead and ascend the North Slopes Route to the summit of "Little Puma." From here, descend 0.3 mile northeast to the 11,100-foot saddle between "Little Puma" and Farnum. Hike 0.3 mile east to Farnum's rocky summit, which offers open views to the west. Trees block what would be a spectacular view of Bison and McCurdy to the northeast.

See map 10, page 80

## 10. "Burntop"    11,085 feet

"Burntop" is 1.9 miles north-northwest of "Little Puma" and 1.0 mile north-northeast of Packer Gulch Trailhead. A gentle ridge connects "Burntop" and "Little Puma." "Burntop" suffered a bad fire, and its summit and ridges are scarred. Nevertheless, it is a ranked peak over 11,000 feet. Even burned, the bristlecone pines on the summit are magnificent. In compensation for the fire, the summit now offers open views. The view of Bison and McCurdy is especially fine.

## Route
### 10.4 South Ridge *Classic*
*From Packer Gulch TH at 9,700 ft:*     65 RP     2.4 mi     1,385 ft     Class 2

This is the easiest route up "Burntop," and it is a wonderful little hike. It is the easiest hike in this book that takes you to the summit of a peak over 11,000 feet. You can promenade through open meadows, then walk a rolling ridge to a unique summit. Start at Packer Gulch Trailhead and hike 0.3 mile east-northeast through aspen groves and open meadows to 10,000 feet. Hike 0.3 mile up a steeper slope and reach the south ridge of "Burntop" at 10,600 feet. Hike 0.3 mile north-northwest through the forest to the edge of the burn at 10,800 feet. It may take you a moment to adjust to the burned landscape ahead, but it has its own charm. Hike 0.3 mile north through burned but still erect bristlecones to the highest point. This summit is a memorable place to lounge on a lazy day. Bison and McCurdy dominate your eastern view, and high peaks float on the western horizon.

# 10. Puma Peak Group Combinations
### 10.5 Three Pumas *Classic*
*From Packer Gulch TH at 9,700 ft:*     139 RP     8.1 mi     2,991 ft     Class 2

See map 10, page 80

This is the easiest way to ascend "Puma Peak," "Little Puma" and Farnum Peak together. After you invest in the ascent to the ridge, you may as well hike all three peaks. Start at Packer Gulch Trailhead and ascend the North Slopes Route to the summit of "Puma Peak." Hike 0.6 mile northeast to the 10,954-foot saddle between "Puma Peak" and "Little Puma." Hike 0.3 mile northeast to the summit of "Little Puma." Descend 0.3 mile northeast to the 11,100-foot saddle between "Little Puma" and Farnum. Hike 0.3 mile east to Farnum's summit. Descend Farnum's West Ridge Route. Reascending "Little Puma" on the return is the hike's last uphill obstacle.

### 10.6 Four Pumas *Classic*
*From Packer Gulch TH at 9,700 ft:*     175 RP     8.7 mi     3,407 ft     Class 2

This tour collects all four peaks in the Puma Peak Group. Follow the Three Pumas Route to the 11,100-foot saddle between "Little Puma" and Farnum on your return from Farnum. The good news is that you do not have to reascend "Little Puma." Even better news is that you can ascend "Burntop" instead. Leave the Three Pumas Route and contour 0.3 mile west-northwest across the north side of "Little Puma." Descend 1.0 mile north-

northwest to the 10,580-foot saddle between "Little Puma" and "Burntop." Hike 0.7 mile north to the summit of "Burntop." Descend the South Ridge Route of "Burntop."

See
map 11,
page 85

# 11. SCHOOLMARM GROUP

| | |
|---|---|
| **Schoolmarm Mountain** | **11,332 feet** |
| **Rishaberger Mountain** | **10,460 feet** |
| **Martland Peak** | **11,289 feet** |

These peaks form the Puma Hills' southern massif. This massif is rougher than the Puma Peak Group, and you will find slower hiking here. There are no trails to the summits. These peaks are a few miles north of U.S. 24, and you can easily approach them from there. In spite of their easy access, the summits seldom see hikers' boots. Your efforts will likely reward you with solitude.

**84**

## Maps

*Required: Glentivar*
*Optional: Sulphur Mountain*

## Trailheads

### Sawdust Gulch Trailhead

This trailhead is at 9,600 feet and provides access to Schoolmarm's west side and Rishaberger's north side. If approaching from the east, go 4.6 miles west on U.S. 24 from the summit of Wilkerson Pass. If approaching from the west, go 10.7 miles east on U.S. 24 from Hartsel. At the old townsite of Glentivar, turn north onto Park County 23, a gravel road, and measure from this point. Go north on Park County 23 for 2.7 miles to a junction. Turn northwest (gentle left) and go northwest then west to another junction at 3.9 miles. Turn northwest onto Turner Gulch Road and enter the Pike National Forest at 4.2 miles. Turner Gulch Road is still Park County 23. Go northwest, north, then northeast on Turner Gulch Road as it curves around the base of Point 10,412, alias "Roachaburger." Turn east (right) onto Sawdust Gulch Road at 6.3 miles. Park here; this is the trailhead. Schoolmarm Mountain is 1.6 miles east.

### Tener Gulch Trailhead

This trailhead is at 9,560 feet and provides access to Martland's south side. If approaching from the east, go 2.3 miles west on U.S. 24 from the summit of Wilkerson Pass. If approaching from the west, go 13.0 miles east on U.S. 24 from Hartsel. Turn north onto Park County 23A, a gravel road, and measure from this point. Go north on Park County 23A, turn northwest

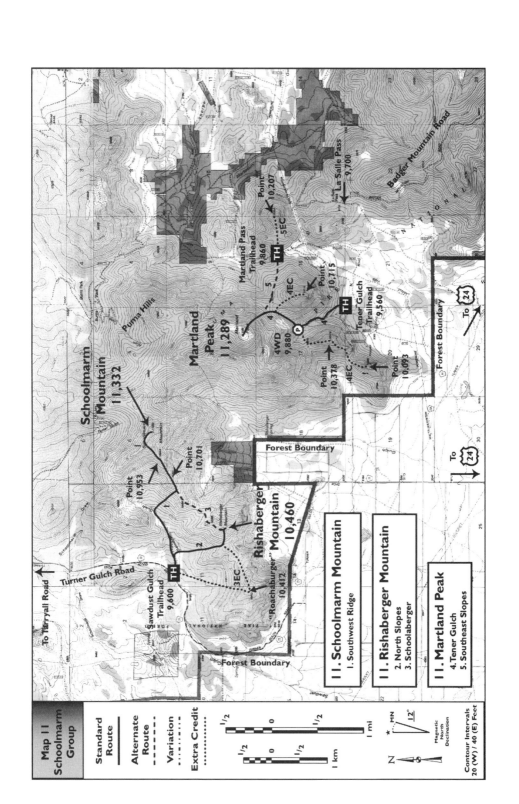

Map 11
Schoolmarm Group

Standard Route
Alternate Route
Variation
Extra Credit

Contour Intervals
20 (W) / 40 (E) Feet

Magnetic North Declination

11. Schoolmarm Mountain
1. Southwest Ridge

11. Rishaberger Mountain
2. North Slopes
3. Schoolaberger

11. Martland Peak
4. Tener Gulch
5. Southeast Slopes

Schoolmarm Mountain 11,332

Martland Peak 11,289

Rishaberger Mountain 10,460

"Rishaberger" 10,412

Point 10,953

Point 10,701

Point 10,715

Point 10,378

Point 10,093

Point 10,207

Puma Hills

Martland Pass Trailhead 9,860

La Salle Pass 9,700

Badger Mountain Road

Tener Gulch Trailhead 9,560

Sawdust Gulch Trailhead 9,600

4WD 9,880

To Tarryall Road

Turner Gulch Road

Forest Boundary

Forest Boundary

Forest Boundary

To 24

To 24

*Schoolmarm Mountain from the north*

(gentle left) at 0.7 mile, go straight (left) at 1.0 mile, turn east (hard right) onto La Salle Pass Road at 2.1 miles, turn northeast (left) at 2.4 miles and enter the Pike National Forest at 2.6 miles. Continue northeast on FS 44.2, turn north (left) at 2.8 miles, go under power lines at mile 2.9 and turn east (right) at mile 3.4. Continue east on FS 44.2, turn east (right) at mile 3.6 and turn north (left) onto FS 44.2D (Tener Gulch Road) at mile 3.75. Go north on Tener Gulch Road and park at mile 3.9 just before the road enters the trees. This is the trailhead.

You can see Martland to the north during your approach to the trailhead, but you cannot see Martland from the trailhead. From the trailhead, four-wheel-drive vehicles can continue 0.6 mile north on Tener Gulch Road to a road junction in a meadow at 9,880 feet.

### Martland Pass Trailhead

This trailhead is at 9,860 feet and provides access to Martland's southeast side. Follow our directions for Tener Gulch Trailhead to the Pike National Forest boundary at mile 2.6. Continue northeast on FS 44.2, turn east (right) onto FS 44.2A at 2.8 miles and reach some power lines at mile 3.2. Turn northeast with the power lines at mile 3.4, go straight through a four-way junction at mile 4.1 and go straight (left) onto FS 229 at mile 4.6 where the power lines go east. Go north on FS 229 and reach the trailhead on Martland Pass at mile 5.0. Martland Pass is the 9,860-foot pass between Point 10,207 to the east and Point 10,715 to the west. From the trailhead, you can see Martland's rounded summit to the northwest.

# 11. Schoolmarm Mountain    11,332 feet

See map 11, page 85

Schoolmarm Mountain is 2.8 miles south of "Puma Peak" and 4.7 miles north of U.S. 24. You can see Schoolmarm from U.S. 24, and its rounded slopes may not inspire you at first glance. Like most schoolteachers, however, the peak has credentials. Schoolmarm Mountain is the fourth-highest peak, the third-highest ranked peak and the highest named, ranked peak in the Puma Hills. If this is not enough, ascend it to see its unique summit view.

87

## Route
### 11.1 Southwest Ridge *Classic*
*From Sawdust Gulch TH at 9,600 ft:    81 RP    3.8 mi    1,920 ft   Class 2*

This is the easiest route on Schoolmarm. It is a rough, rewarding bushwhack. Start at Sawdust Gulch Trailhead and hike 0.7 mile east up Sawdust Gulch to 9,960 feet. Leave Sawdust Gulch and hike south on an old road. When the road turns back to the north, continue south and reach Schoolmarm's southwest ridge at 10,500 feet. Hike 0.7 mile northeast on this interesting ridge, crossing Points 10,701 and 10,953 en route, and reach Schoolmarm's northwest ridge at 11,260 feet. Hike 100 yards southeast to the summit. From here, you can survey the Southern Puma Hills to the south, South Tarryall Peak to the east-northeast and McCurdy Mountain to the northeast.

# 11. Rishaberger Mountain    10,460 feet

See map 11, page 85

Rishaberger Mountain is 1.4 miles southwest of Schoolmarm Mountain. Rishaberger does not rank, but it has other redeeming features. The peak is rocky and rough. The short hike to the summit requires a dedicated effort.

## Route
### 11.2 North Slopes
*From Sawdust Gulch TH at 9,600 ft:    38 RP    2.0 mi    860 ft   Class 2*

This is the shortest route on Rishaberger and one of the shortest hikes in this book. Start at Sawdust Gulch Trailhead and hike 0.2 mile east up Sawdust Gulch. Leave Sawdust Gulch and hike 0.6 mile south-southeast up a shallow gully to 10,100 feet on Rishaberger's west ridge. Hike 0.2 mile east up a rough slope to the summit. Locating the highest point is a challenge, as there are several little outcrops to choose from.

*Rishaberger Mountain from the southeast*

See
map 11,
page 85

## 11. Schoolmarm and Rishaberger Combination

### 11.3 Schoolaberger

*From Sawdust Gulch TH at 9,600 ft:    102 RP      4.4 mi      2,261 ft    Class 2*

This is the easiest way to ascend Schoolmarm and Rishaberger together. Start at Sawdust Gulch Trailhead and ascend Schoolmarm's Southwest Ridge Route. From Schoolmarm's summit, descend Schoolmarm's southwest ridge all the way to the 10,220-foot Schoolmarm-Rishaberger saddle. Hike 0.1 mile southwest to Rishaberger's 10,366-foot false summit. Continue 0.2 mile southwest over rough ground to the summit. Descend Rishaberger's North Slopes Route.

### 11.3EC Extra Credit Recess—"Roachaburger" 10,412 feet *Classic*

*From Sawdust Gulch TH at 9,600 ft:    123 RP      5.1 mi      2,653 ft    Class 2*

Point 10,412, alias "Roachaburger," is 0.7 mile west-southwest of Rishaberger. "Roachaburger" is a ranked peak. Adding it to the tour completes your school lesson. On your descent of Rishaberger's North Slopes Route, continue down Rishaberger's west ridge to the 10,020-foot saddle between Rishaberger and "Roachaburger." Hike 0.4 mile west to the summit of "Roachaburger." Stay north of a 10,340-foot false summit en route. The summit of "Roachaburger" is better defined than Rishaberger's, but there is

"Roachaburger"
10,412

89

*"Roachaburger" from the southeast*

little view. Descend 0.9 mile north to Sawdust Gulch Trailhead. There is a lot of deadfall on this slope.

# 11. Martland Peak     11,289 feet

See map 11, page 85

Martland Peak is 1.5 miles southeast of Schoolmarm Mountain and 3.7 miles north of U.S. 24. Like Schoolmarm, Martland is a ranked elevener and has no trail to its rough summit. Enjoy the wild summits while they last. Martland has four ranked 10,000-foot summits south of it. The four Teners, as we call them, may bring a tenuous aria to your lips, and they will certainly extend your otherwise modest Martland adventure. This is a petite peak playground.

## Routes
### 11.4 Tener Gulch *Classic*
*From Tener Gulch TH at 9,560 ft:*     62 RP     3.0 mi     1,729 ft     Class 2
*From 4WD parking at 9,880 ft:*     50 RP     1.8 mi     1,409 ft     Class 2

This is Martland's easiest route, and it is an easier hike than School-marm's Southwest Ridge Route. Start at Tener Gulch Trailhead and go 0.6 mile north on Tener Gulch Road to a road junction in a meadow at 9,880 feet. Leave the road here and hike 0.4 mile northeast on faint game trails toward the 10,262-foot pass between Martland to the north and Point

Martland Peak Labels: **Martland Peak 11,289**, **Point 10,715**, **Point 10,378**

*Martland Peak from the south*

10,715 to the south (Class 1). There is a large grove of small aspen trees in the pass that is difficult to hike through. To avoid the difficulty, turn northwest toward Martland before you reach the pass. Hike 0.5 mile northwest up a rough slope to the summit (Class 2). From the summit, you have peekaboo views through the trees of Bison and McCurdy to the northeast.

### 11.4EC Extra Credit Three Teners—Points 10,715, 10,378 and 10,093

From the 10,292-foot saddle, hike 0.4 mile south to the summit of Point 10,715 (Class 2). For more credit, return to the saddle and hike 0.6 mile southwest to Point 10,378 (Class 2). For a clean sweep, continue 0.5 mile southwest to Point 10,093. Prepare yourself for a surprise ending. Point 10,093, the lowest of the four Teners, does not yield easily. It is a Class 5 rock climb.

### 11.5 Southeast Slopes

*From Martland Pass TH at 9,860 ft:*　　63 RP　　2.0 mi　　1,429 ft　　Class 2

This is the shortest route on Martland. You start higher than Tener Gulch Trailhead, but this hike is entirely Class 2. Start at Martland Pass Trailhead. Martland is only 1.0 mile to the northwest, but the northern slopes of Point 10,715, the highest of the four Teners, are between you and Martland. From Martland Pass, hike 0.5 mile west to the 10,292-foot saddle between Point 10,715 and Martland. Traversing this north-facing slope is the route's crux. From the 10,292-foot saddle, join the South Slopes Route and hike 0.5 mile northwest up a rough slope to Martland's summit.

### 11.5EC Extra Credit—Point 10,207

From Martland Pass, hike 0.4 mile east to the summit of Point 10,207 (Class 2). If you did not climb Point 10,093 on Route 11.4EC, you can complete your three Teners here.

## 12. Badger Mountain 11,294 feet

Badger Mountain is 1.0 mile northeast of Wilkerson Pass and U.S. 24. Badger has a forest of electronic equipment on its summit, and that is a sign that we have completed our tour across the Retirement Range. We include Badger because it is prominent and to complete our coverage of all the ranked eleveners in the Puma Hills.

91

See
map 12,
page 92

### Maps

*Required: Glentivar*
*Optional: Tarryall*

### Trailhead

#### Wilkerson Pass Trailhead

This trailhead is at 9,500 feet and provides access to Badger's south side. Wilkerson Pass is on U.S. 24, 23.0 miles west of Divide and 15.3 miles east

Badger Mountain
11,294

*Badger Mountain from the north*

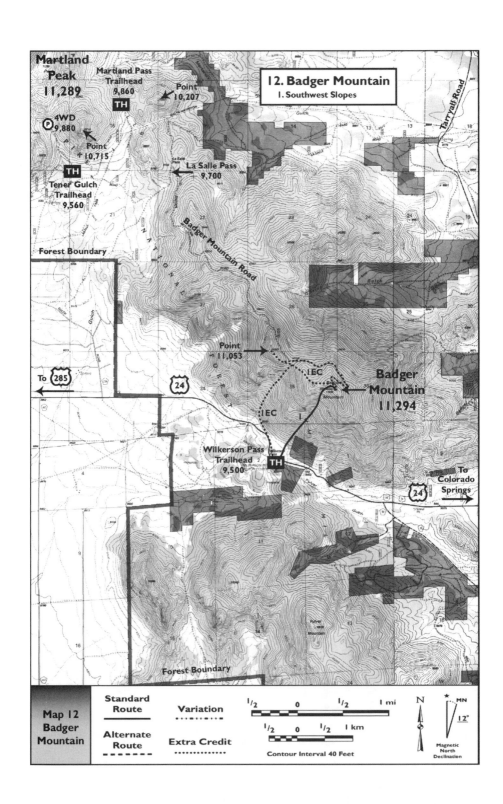

Martland
Peak
11,289

Martland Pass
Trailhead
9,860
**TH**

Point
10,207

Ⓟ 4WD
9,880

Point
10,715

**TH**

Tener Gulch
Trailhead
9,560

La Salle Pass
9,700

Forest Boundary

Badger Mountain Road

**12. Badger Mountain**
1. Southwest Slopes

Tarryall Road

Gulch

NATIONAL

FOREST

Point
11,053

1EC

Badger
Mountain
11,294

To 285

24

1EC

Wilkerson Pass
Trailhead
9,500

**TH**

To
Colorado
Springs

24

Forest Boundary

| Map 12<br>Badger<br>Mountain | Standard<br>Route | Variation | | | |
| --- | --- | --- | --- | --- | --- |
| | Alternate<br>Route | Extra Credit | | | |

½    0    ½    1 mi

½    0    ½    1 km

Contour Interval 40 Feet

N

★ MN

12°

Magnetic
North
Declination

of Hartsel. Park in the Forest Service visitor center parking lot on the south side of the highway. This trailhead is accessible in winter.

## Route

### 12.1 Southwest Slopes
*From Wilkerson Pass TH at 9,500 ft:*    *73 RP*    *2.0 mi*    *1,794 ft*   *Class 2*

This is the shortest route on Badger. It is one of the steepest routes in the Puma Hills. Start at Wilkerson Pass Trailhead and cross to the north side of U.S. 24. Hike 1.0 mile southeast to the summit. Fortunately, Badger's highest point has no tower on it; it is 100 yards east of the easternmost and largest tower. For information about the electronic equipment on Badger's summit, call the Forest Service at (719) 836-2031 or the station manager at (719) 545-8737.

### 12.1EC Extra Credit—Point 11,053
To end our journey on a wild summit and complete a sweep of the eleveners in the Puma Hills, hike 0.9 mile northwest from Badger's summit to Point 11,053 (Class 2).

*Ah! The clock is always slow;*
*It is later than you think.*

—Robert Service

*chapter five*

# Super Hikes

## Introduction

In case you are about to put this book down because all these hikes are too short, keep reading. Super Hikes in the Retirement Range are for those training for long races or other endurance events. Traversing these linear ranges is an obvious challenge. We describe a traverse for each range and a grand traverse that ascends every peak in this book. These routes will tease, test, then torment you. Afterward, maybe you will feel good about what you have done. The secret Roach formula for Super Hiking is simple: Go like hell. Go now, feel like hell later.

*A Classic Summit Hike*

# 13. PLATTE RIVER MOUNTAINS SUPER HIKES

The Platte River Mountains are all lined up for the taking. Take them. The easiest version of this event starts at Kenosha Pass Trailhead and finishes at Brookside-Payne Trailhead. You will need to arrange a vehicle shuttle between these two trailheads.

## Maps

*Required: Mount Logan, Shawnee, Topaz Mountain, Windy Peak*
*Optional: Bailey*

## Routes

### 13.1 Platte Master *Classic*

*OW from Kenosha Pass TH at 10,060 ft:   461 RP 25.1 mi  5,525 ft Class 2*
*OW from Brookside-Payne TH at 8,020 ft:526 RP 25.1 mi  7,565 ft Class 2*
*RT from either TH:                987 RP 50.2 mi 13,090 ft Class 2*

The route is along the range crest, and most of the traverse has been covered in earlier descriptions. Get your maps out. Starting at Kenosha Pass Trailhead, ascend nine summits in the following order: North Twin Cone, Blaine, South Twin Cone, Foster Benchmark, "Platte Peak," Shawnee, "No Payne," Payne Benchmark and "Lost Platte Peak." If this is not enough, start at Brookside-Payne Trailhead and finish at Kenosha Pass Trailhead. The distance is the same, but the elevation gain is more. If you are still not tired, do the round trip. For this event, you will not need a vehicle shuttle!

# 14. KENOSHA MOUNTAINS SUPER HIKES

There is always more. Keep reading. Traversing the Kenosha Mountains is an event for the fit. The easiest version of this event starts at South Ben Tyler Trailhead and finishes at Stoney Pass Trailhead. You will need to arrange a vehicle shuttle between these two trailheads.

## Maps

*Required: Mount Logan, Topaz Mountain, Windy Peak, Green Mountain*
*Optional: Observatory Rock, Shawnee, Cheesman Lake*

## Routes

### 14.1 Kinetic Kenosher *Classic*

*OW from South Ben Tyler TH at 9,760 ft:560 RP 26.5 mi  7,837 ft  Class 2*
*OW from Stoney Pass TH at 8,562 ft:    642 RP  26.5 mi  9,357 ft  Class 2*
*RT from either TH:              1,202 RP 53.0 mi 17,194 ft Class 2*

*On "Peak X"*

This is the toughest of the four single-range Super Hikes. Trim the borders off your maps to save weight. Bravo if you do it in one day. You can do it in two days with a resupply and car camp at Lost Park Campground, next to Lost Park Trailhead. The easiest version of this event starts at South Ben Tyler Trailhead and finishes at Stoney Pass Trailhead, and that is how we describe it.

Starting at South Ben Tyler Trailhead, do Alphabetizer over the summits of "Kenosha Peak," "X-Prime," "Peak X," "Peak Y," "Peak Z," and "Zephyr." From the summit of "Zephyr," descend 1.0 mile to the Colorado Trail on the north side of the North Fork of Lost Creek at 10,560 feet. Hike (or run) 3.2 miles southeast on the Colorado Trail to 10,240 feet. You can escape the traverse at this point (see Route 14.1V).

For the rest of the traverse, continue 1.8 miles east on the Colorado Trail to the 10,460-foot saddle between Windy Peak and the Peak X Group. Leave the trail here. Hike 1.0 mile southeast to 11,200 feet, then 0.4 mile east to the broad 11,246-foot saddle on Windy Peak's West Ridge Route. Follow that route to the summit of Windy Peak. Descend Windy Peak's East Ridge Route to the 10,660-foot saddle between Windy Peak and Buffalo Peak. Ascend the top part of Buffalo's West Ridge Route to Buffalo's summit and descend Buffalo's Northeast Slopes Route to Stoney Pass Trailhead.

### 14.1V Variation

*OW from South Ben Tyler TH at 9,760 ft:581 RP 27.2 mi 8,057 ft Class 2*
*End at Lost Park TH at 9,980 ft:         285 RP 15.9 mi 4,424 ft Class 2*
*OW from Stoney Pass TH at 8,562 ft:     656 RP 27.2 mi 9,617 ft Class 2*
*End at Lost Park TH at 9,980 ft:         325 RP 11.3 mi 5,413 ft Class 2*
*RT from either TH:                     1,236 RP 54.4 mi 17,674 ft Class 2*

You can visit Lost Park Trailhead in the middle of the traverse. You can either plan to do this or use this variation as an escape route. If you are going from west to east, you can leave the traverse from the Colorado Trail 3.2 miles southeast of the point where you reached the trail after descending "Zephyr." Cross to the creek's south side and hike 2.0 miles southeast then south on a spur trail to Lost Park Trailhead. To continue the west-to-east traverse, ascend Windy Peak's complete West Ridge Route. If you are going east to west, reverse this two-step visitation process.

# 15. TARRYALL MOUNTAINS SUPER HIKES

There is always more. Keep reading. Traversing the Tarryall Mountains is another event for the fit. If you do all these traverses, perhaps fame will follow. The easiest version of this event starts at Lost Pass Trailhead and finishes at Spruce Grove Trailhead. You will need to arrange a vehicle shuttle between these two trailheads.

*McCurdy Mountain from Badger Mountain*

## Maps

Required: Topaz Mountain, Farnum Peak, McCurdy Mountain
Optional: Observatory Rock, Windy Peak

## Routes

### 15.1 Tarrynot *Classic*

OW from Lost Pass TH at 10,670 ft:        500 RP   23.7 mi    7,384 ft   Class 2
OW from Spruce Grove TH at 8,560 ft: 546 RP   23.7 mi    9,494 ft   Class 2
RT from either TH:                         1,046 RP   47.4 mi  16,878 ft   Class 2

Tarrynot tallies all Tarryalls. Keep your maps out. This hike is between the Platte Master and Kinetic Kenosher in difficulty. Start at Lost Pass Trailhead and ascend North Tarryall Peak's North Slopes Route. Traverse 2.5 miles southeast to Topaz. To do this, reverse the description given with Route 6.3 No Tarry Top. The 5.6-mile bushwhack from the summit of Topaz to Bison Pass is the crux of the traverse. Tarry not.

Hike 1.0 mile southeast to Point 11,663 on top of Hourglass Burn. From here, descend 1.0 mile southeast to a 11,220-foot saddle. Stay north of Point 11,523 en route. From the saddle, hike 0.6 mile southeast to Point 11,611. This is a ranked elevener, and now is your chance to ascend it. From Point 11,611, navigate carefully as you hike 1.8 miles southeast to an 11,140-foot saddle 0.7 mile south-southwest of Point 11,469. Navigate carefully as you continue 0.5 mile east over rough terrain to an 11,100-foot saddle. This,

*A Tarryall afternoon*

not Bison Pass, is the low point between Topaz and Bison. Persevere and hike 0.7 mile southeast to Bison Pass at 11,180 feet. Your life will be better for a while.

Follow the upper part of Bison's Southwest Ridge Route to Bison's summit. Return to Bison Arm and follow the upper part of McCurdy's West Slopes Route to McCurdy's summit. Descend McCurdy's South Slopes Route to the trail junction with the Lake Park Trail in a small saddle at 10,740 feet. Leave the Brookside-McCurdy Trail, turn east (left) onto the Lake Park Trail and hike east and south on it 3.0 miles through Lake Park to Hankins Pass, climbing "Tarryall Peak" and "Lake Park Peak" en route. Follow the upper part of South Tarryall Peak's North Slopes Route. Descend South Tarryall's Southwest Slopes Route to Spruce Grove Trailhead.

# 16. Puma Hills Super Hikes

Like the higher ranges, the Puma Hills offer you a chance to do more than stretch your legs. These hikes will test and reward you. The Puma Hills Super Hikes are the easiest of the four single-range traverses.

## Maps
*Required: Farnum Peak, Glentivar, Pike National Forest*
*Optional: Eagle Rock*

## Trailheads
### Wilkerson Pass–Packer Gulch Connection
For a one-way trip, you need to arrange a vehicle shuttle between Wilkerson Pass and Packer Gulch Trailheads. To do this, go from Wilkerson Pass to Sawdust Gulch Trailhead (see Schoolmarm Group). From here, go 8.9 miles north on Park County 23 (Turner Gulch Road), turn south onto FS 144 (Packer Gulch Road) and go 4.0 miles south to Packer Gulch Trailhead.

## Routes
### 16.1 Eight Pumas *Classic*
*OW from Packer Gulch TH at 9,700 ft: 410 RP 17.3 mi 7,135 ft Class 2*
*OW from Wilkerson Pass TH at 9,500 ft: 428 RP 17.3 mi 7,335 ft Class 2*
*RT from either TH: 838 RP 34.6 mi 14,470 ft Class 2*

This hike ascends all eight eleveners in the Puma Hills. It is a rough but reasonable tour. You can start at either Packer Gulch or Wilkerson Pass Trailhead. These trailheads are close to the same elevation, so the direction you choose does not make much difference. There is 200 feet less gain if you start at Packer Gulch Trailhead. Starting at Wilkerson Pass allows you to ascend Badger's steep south slopes when you are fresh. We describe the route from Packer Gulch Trailhead.

Start at Packer Gulch Trailhead and follow the Four Pumas Route backward, ascending "Burntop," Farnum Peak, "Little Puma" and "Puma Peak." This effort collects half the peaks, but your fun has just begun. From the summit of "Puma Peak," hike 3.6 miles south along the ridge to Schoolmarm. Cross Point 11,143, Point 11,083 and Point 11,065 en route. This is your chance to visit these unranked summits. The low point on the ridge between "Puma Peak" and Schoolmarm is 10,700 feet. From Schoolmarm, hike 2.0 miles east then south to Martland. This is a rough ridge. Descend Martland's Southeast Slopes Route to Martland Pass between Point 10,207 and Point 10,715. Hike 1.0 mile southeast through a 9,820-foot saddle to La Salle Pass at 9,700 feet. Hike 2.3 miles south-southeast on Badger Mountain Road to a 10,671-foot saddle. This is the only Class 1 hiking on the route. Leave the road and hike 0.4 mile south-southeast up the ridge to Point 11,053. Hike 0.9 mile southeast to Badger's summit and descend Badger's Southwest Slopes Route to Wilkerson Pass.

# 17. RETIREMENT RANGE SUPER HIKE

Keep reading. This is the big one, the route that takes you to almost every peak in this book. This is not a training hike. It is the hike. Many people consider the Hardrock 100 endurance event in Colorado's San Juans to be the toughest 100-mile race in America. Arguably, this event is even tougher. Never say that an event is impossible, though. Some like it tough.

## Maps

*Required: Mount Logan, Shawnee, Topaz Mountain, Windy Peak, Green Mountain, Observatory Rock, McCurdy Mountain, Farnum Peak, Glentivar, Cheesman Lake*
*Optional: Eagle Rock, Bailey*

## Route

### 17.1 Out of Retirement *Classic*

*OW from Kenosha Pass TH at 10,060 ft:*

| | | | | |
|---|---|---|---|---|
| *Part 1:* | *810 RP* | *41.6 mi* | *11,284 ft* | *Class 2* |
| *Part 2:* | *300 RP* | *13.1 mi* | *4,634 ft* | *Class 2* |
| *Part 3:* | *551 RP* | *25.3 mi* | *8,207 ft* | *Class 2* |
| *Part 4:* | *640 RP* | *41.4 mi* | *10,398 ft* | *Class 2* |
| *Total:* | *2,419 RP* | *121.4 mi* | *34,523 ft* | *Class 2* |

This Super Hike ascends all but two of the peaks in this book. Bravos if you are still reading. We wish you fame, glory and fortune if you actually do this hike. The easiest version of it starts at Kenosha Pass Trailhead and ends at Observatory Rock Trailhead. That is how we describe it. With some variations to minimize backtracking, the hike tackles the four ranges in order: the Platte River Mountains, the Kenosha Mountains, the Tarryall Mountains and the Puma Hills. The route goes southeast along one range and northwest along the next.

Part 1 covers the Platte River Mountains and two important peaks in the Kenosha Mountains. This is the toughest segment, and it is appropriate for it to be at the beginning. Start at Kenosha Pass Trailhead and follow the Platte Master over North Twin Cone, Blaine, South Twin Cone and Foster Benchmark to Platosha. Instead of hiking directly from Platosha to Little Platosha, ascend "Kenosha Peak" en route. It is important to summit "Kenosha Peak" now to avoid route inefficiencies later. From Little Platosha, continue on Platte Master over "Platte Peak," Shawnee, "No Payne," Payne Benchmark and "Lost Platte Peak." From the summit of "Lost Platte Peak," descend 0.6 mile southwest and reach the Payne Creek Trail at 9,400 feet. Follow the Payne Creek Trail 3.4 miles southeast to the Colorado Trail at 9,300 feet. Ascend the upper part of Windy Peak's North Ridge Route to Windy's summit. Descend Windy's East Ridge Route to the 10,660-foot saddle between Windy and Buffalo. Ascend the top part of Buffalo's West Ridge Route to Buffalo's summit and return to the 10,660-foot saddle. Descend 1.2 miles south on the Rolling Creek Trail to a trail junction with the Wigwam Trail at 9,620 feet. Hike 6.8 miles west on the Wigwam Trail to Lost Park Trailhead and Campground, where you can be met by vehicles and take a break.

Part 2 finishes the Kenosha Mountains. This is the easiest segment. Continue on the second part of the east-to-west version of Kinetic Kenosher (Route 14.1V). Ascend "Zephyr," "Peak Z," "Peak Y," "Peak X," and "X-Prime." From the summit of "X-Prime," return via the descent described with Route 4.3EC to 10,800 feet. Hike 0.3 mile southeast to 10,900-foot North Lost Pass. Hike 0.8 mile southeast to Point 11,270, a bonus peak. Descend 0.7 mile to Lost Pass Trailhead, where you can receive vehicle support.

Part 3 covers the Tarryall Mountains. This segment, although only part of this event, does rival the Pikes Peak Marathon. Do the west-to-east version of Tarrynot over North Tarryall, Topaz, Bison, McCurdy, "Tarryall Peak," "Lake Park Peak" and South Tarryall to Spruce Grove Trailhead, where you can receive vehicle support.

Part 4 covers the Puma Hills. This is the second-hardest segment, but you finish on easy terrain. From Spruce Grove Trailhead, you have to cover 10.9 road miles to reach the Puma Hills. Hike 1.6 miles south on Park

*"Peak X" from North Tarryall Peak*

County 77 (Tarryall Road) to Park County 31. Hike 2.3 miles south on Park County 31 to Park County 44 (La Salle Pass Road). Hike 3.9 miles west on Park County 44 to La Salle Pass. Hike 3.1 miles south-southeast on Badger Mountain Road to a 10,740-foot saddle. Leave the road and hike 0.6 mile southeast to Badger Mountain's summit. Your transition to the Puma Hills is complete. From Badger's summit, follow the south-to-north version of Eight Pumas over Martland, Schoolmarm, "Puma Peak," "Little Puma," Farnum and "Burntop" to Packer Gulch Trailhead, where you can receive vehicle support.

Two peaks to go. To escape Packer Gulch and ascend Eagle and Observatory Rocks, you have some more road miles to do. You can have vehicle support with you for most of this distance. You can also preview this part of the course by vehicle. From Packer Gulch Trailhead, hike 0.4 mile west on FS 144 (Packer Gulch Road) to the first switchback. Leave FS 144 and hike 1.0 mile west-northwest on FS 209A to FS 209 (West Packer Road). Hike 1.2 miles west on FS 209 to FS 145 in Turner Gulch. Hike 1.7 miles north on FS 145 to Park County 23 (Turner Gulch Road). Hike 0.4 mile northwest on Park County 23 and turn northwest (right) onto FS 146. Hike 0.8 mile northwest then west on FS 146, descend into Ruby Gulch, turn south-southwest (left) and hike 0.3 mile south to East Eagle Rock Trailhead. Ascend Eagle Rock's North Ridge Route and descend the Southwest Ridge Route to West Eagle Rock Trailhead.

*Why we train. Gerry on top of King Peak, June 1999.*
*(photo by Mike Butyn)*

One peak to go. Hike 1.4 miles west on FS 146 to FS 148. Go 0.2 mile straight on FS 148 to FS 834. Go 2.4 miles north then west on FS 834 to FS 148 (Observatory Rock Road). Hike 0.3 mile west to the four-wheel-drive park south of Observatory Rock. Ascend Observatory Rock's South Slopes Route. Review your work. Descend Observatory Rock's South Slopes Route to Observatory Rock Trailhead, where hikers can stop hiking and readers can stop reading.

*An owl sat once with his sharp hearing,*
  *his watchfulness,*
    *his bill, half-grown, majestic on my finger;*
*then I felt his huge and yellow stare*
*plant something foreign in me,*
  *a deep quiet,*
*a mad freedom; my heart laughed*
  *when the bird raised his soft wings.*

—Thorkild Bjornvig

# APPENDIX

## In Defense of Mountaineering Guidebooks
*by Gerry Roach*

I am always amazed when I see stumps of once-large trees near treeline. They are not going to grow back, at least not until a comet hits Earth and changes the balance of nature. I am equally amazed that nothing grows on mine tailings. Even a comet may not make them fertile. We are the future generation, and we have stumps and tailings to look at. Yet the mountains are not dead. We can climb them, then loll about in fields of flowers.

Ironically, we now drive up the miners' old roads in four-wheel-drive vehicles made of mined metals, hike uphill for a few hours to a summit and claim a personal victory or conquest. Miners and loggers make physical extractions from the mountains. Climbers make mental extractions from the mountains. For now, we have driven mining and logging offshore. We no longer rush to the mountains to get the gold, we go to get their good tidings.

A debate today swirls around the opinion that even climbers' mental extractions are causing unacceptable environmental damage. We leave too many footprints. Those who choose to make an effort are being cast as pseudocriminals who love the mountains to death. Eh? I take a longer view. Death to a mountain is when it is mined into oblivion like Bartlett Mountain. Death to a mountain is when it commits suicide like Mount St. Helens. As violent as those actions were, we can still climb the stumps of those peaks. There are still good tidings there.

Any long view must compare the damage done by hikers' boots with that caused by monster trucks. Obviously, boots pale in comparison. Still, are boots too much? Sometimes, yes. What do we do? Rather than lament the lost age when we could walk unfettered by such concerns, we should strap in and solve the problem. For a government agency to shut the door and refuse entry is not a solution. Excess footprints are easily dealt with. We need sustainable trails through the fragile zones. The Colorado Fourteener Initiative is creating these trails on Colorado's Fourteeners. Their efforts are a grand example of the public's ability to strap in and solve the problem. There is no environmental problem created by hikers that cannot be solved by hikers.

*The summit of Bison Peak*

Our mental extractions from the mountains are going to continue to increase. So is the positive social value of these gifts. As society creaks and groans in other arenas, we need the mountains' good tidings more than ever. The gift that mountains offer society is immense. Mountains give us an arena where we can lift not just our bodies but our spirits. Without uplifted spirits, we devolve. Mountaineering is a great metaphor for life and, like life, it is worth fighting for. I view guidebooks as part of the solution, not part of the problem.

I started climbing in 1955. For nearly 20 years, I could not conceive of writing a guidebook. I reasoned, like a miner, that the good tidings were hidden and that, once found, they should be protected by a claim. I felt a proprietary ownership of the secrets I found through my efforts. I felt that sharing the secret would diminish it as a microscope can change the microbe. I dashed across the globe to discover it before it was diminished. Although I had many unique climbs and experiences, this effort left me frustrated and exhausted. I could not dash fast enough. Too many people were ahead of me. After an ascent of the Matterhorn in 1973 that I shared with a hundred other people, I pointed to the heavens and started pontificating about the lost age. Then I realized no one was listening. They were just climbing the Matterhorn. Society had jumped my claim. I pondered this for many years.

Still, I did not write a guidebook. I reasoned that sharing would attract still more people to these precious areas and hasten their demise. I clung to this view as the population quietly doubled and mountain use increased tenfold. My pontifical finger withered. I was alone with my memories of the lost age. Then, early one morning in 1981, I sat upright in bed and started writing a guidebook. It was done in a week. At the time I could not explain it, but I suddenly knew that not sharing would hasten the demise. Finally, I just set the demise aside. I knew that what the mountains needed was love.

Approached with love, the mountains can endure our mental extractions forever. Approached with malice, greed or ignorance, the mountains will indeed suffer. Worse, even with love, hikers may lose their access because of other interests and opinions. The government agencies and monster trucks stand ready. The best we can do is love the mountains and share this love. Hikers as a group need to evolve. We must spread our arms wide and embrace not just the mountains but other user groups as well. The mountains need ambassadors—loving user groups who are intimate with the mountains' secrets. I offer my guidebooks from a deep love for the mountains so that future ambassadors can also share the mountains' good tidings.

## Map Information

We have written this book to be used with good maps. We recommend the 7.5-minute USGS topographic quadrangles. They are available in many shops and at the Map Sales Office in the Denver Federal Center; call (303) 236-7477 for information. You can mail-order maps from the Federal Center, but they will not accept telephone orders. All the quadrangles referred to in this book are 7.5-minute quadrangles. The nontopographic Pike National Forest map is also useful; it gives you the big picture and has more current road information than the USGS quadrangles. For the same reasons, the topographic Trails Illustrated map 105 for the Tarryall Mountains and Kenosha Pass is useful. Check www.trailsillustrated.com for information on Trails Illustrated maps. We list the required and optional USGS quadrangles with each peak or group of peaks and in the following shopping list.

### SHOPPING LIST FOR USGS QUADRANGLES
(† *means required*)

| | |
|---|---|
| †Bailey | †McCurdy Mountain |
| Cheesman Lake | Milligan Lakes |
| †Eagle Rock | †Mount Logan |
| Elkhorn | †Observatory Rock |
| †Farnum Peak | Pine |
| †Glentivar | †Shawnee |
| †Green Mountain | †Sulphur Mountain |
| Hackett Mountain | Tarryall |
| Hartsel | †Topaz Mountain |
| Jefferson | †Windy Peak |

"Puma Peak"
11,570

"Little Puma"
11,449

*"On top of Farnum Peak"*

# *Classic* Hikes

## Platte River Mountains

| | |
|---|---|
| South Twin Cone Peak | 1.5 South Slopes |
| Twin Cones and Blaine Combination | 1.6 Cone Master |
| "Platte Peak" | 2.1 North Slopes |
| "Platte Peak" and Shawnee Combination | 2.4 Platte Plus |
| "No Payne" | 3.1 Northeast Slopes |
| Payne Benchmark | 3.2 Northwest Slopes |

## Kenosha Mountains

| | |
|---|---|
| "Kenosha Peak" | 4.1 South Slopes |
| "Peak X" | 4.4 Southeast Slopes |
| "Peak Y" | 4.5 West Slopes |
| "Peak Z" | 4.6 South Ridge |
| "Zephyr" | 4.7 Southwest Slopes |
| Peaks X, Y, Z and Zephyr Combination | 4.9 Alphabetizer |
| Windy Peak | 5.1 West Ridge |
| Buffalo Mountain | 5.6 West Ridge |
| The Castle | 5.7 Southeast Gully |

## Tarryall Mountains

| | |
|---|---|
| North Tarryall and Topaz Combination | 6.3 No Tarry Top |
| Bison Peak | 7.1 Southwest Ridge |
| Bison Peak | 7.2 Northwest Slopes |
| McCurdy Mountain | 7.3 South Slopes |
| McCurdy Mountain | 7.4 West Slopes |
| Bison and McCurdy Combination | 7.5 McBison |
| "Tarryall Peak" North Slopes | 8.1 North Slopes |
| South Tarryall Peak | 8.3 North Slopes |

## Puma Hills

| | |
|---|---|
| Observatory Rock | 9.1 South Slopes |
| Eagle Rock | 9.3 North Ridge |
| "Puma Peak" | 10.1 North Slopes |
| "Burntop" | 10.4 South Ridge |
| "Puma Peak" to Farnum Combination | 10.5 Three Pumas |
| "Puma Peak" to "Burntop" Combination | 10.6 Four Pumas |
| Schoolmarm | 11.1 Southwest Ridge |
| "Roachaburger" | 11.3 EC Recess |
| Martland | 11.4 Tener Gulch |

*All the Super Hikes are super-classic. Good luck!*

# PEAK LISTS

The following lists cover each individual range and the combination of all four ranges that we call the Retirement Range.

A peak qualifies for a list if it is in the area covered by the list and the peak is named or ranked. Named summits are on the list whether or not they are ranked. The officially named summits include peaks, mounts, mountains, named ridges, named benchmarks if they do not have a peak name, named rocks and named hills. Unofficial names are enclosed in quotes in the text but not in the lists. If a summit has both a peak name and a named benchmark, the peak name takes precedence.

We list ranked summits whether or not they are named. We rank a summit if it rises at least 300 feet from the highest connecting saddle to a higher, ranked summit. The closest higher, ranked summit is the parent. A fine point is that this may be a different peak than the higher, ranked summit above the highest connecting saddle. Our list differs from other lists in that we search for a higher, ranked parent, not any peak on the list, which may be lower and unranked.

A peak has a "hard rank" if its summit rises at least 300 feet from its highest connecting saddle to a higher, ranked summit. Summits with a hard rank have a rank number on the right side of the Rank column. Rank numbers increase with decreasing elevation and are for the given list only. The rank calculation is based on given elevations for the summit and saddle if they are available.

We give interpolated elevations to summits and saddles that are shown only with contour lines. Most USGS quadrangles covering this area have 40-foot contour intervals. On these quadrangles, we add 20 feet to the elevation of the highest closed contour for a summit without a given elevation, and give unmarked saddles an elevation halfway between the highest contour that does not go through the saddle and the lowest contour that does go through the saddle. For quadrangles with a 20-foot contour interval, we add 10 feet to the elevation of the highest closed contour for a summit without a given elevation.

Summits that do not have a hard rank, but could rank if interpolated elevations were not used for either the summit or connecting saddle, have a "soft rank." These summits have an S on the left side of the Rank column but no rank number.

It is interesting to be on a summit and know where the nearest higher peak is. The Parent column gives the name of the parent peak, and the Mile column gives the straight-line distance in miles to the parent peak. The Quadrangle column gives the USGS 7.5-minute quadrangle that shows the peak's summit. The parent may be on a different quadrangle. We use the following abbreviations: Pk for Peak, Mt for Mount, Mtn for Mountain, BM for Benchmark.

112

## Colorado's Platte River Mountains
### PLATTE RIVER MOUNTAINS–SORTED BY ELEVATION

| Rank | Elev. | Summit Name | Parent | Mile | Rise | Quadrangle |
|------|-------|-------------|--------|------|------|------------|
| 1 | 12,340 | South Twin Cone Pk | Pk X | 5.2 | 720 | Mt Logan |
| 2 | 12,323 | North Twin Cone Pk | South Twin Cone Pk | 1.4 | 383 | Mt Logan |
|  | 12,303 | Blaine, Mt | South Twin Cone Pk | 1.0 | 203 | Mt Logan |
| 3 | 11,941 | Platte Pk | Kenosha Pk | 1.3 | 401 | Shawnee |
| 4 | 11,927 | Shawnee Pk | Platte Pk | 1.3 | 307 | Shawnee |
|  | 11,871 | Foster BM | South Twin Cone Pk | 1.4 | 211 | Mt Logan |
| 5 | 11,789 | No Payne | Shawnee Pk | 1.9 | 369 | Shawnee |
| 6 | 11,780 | Payne BM | No Payne | 1.5 | 520 | Topaz Mtn |
| 7 | 10,657 | Lost Platte Pk | Point 11,271 | 3.1 | 767 | Windy Pk |
| 8 | 10,190 | Point 10,190 | South Twin Cone Pk | 4.4 | 307 | Observatory Rock |
|  | 9,300 | Mud Hill | Point 9,928 | 1.7 | 80 | Observatory Rock |
|  | 8,220 | Insmont Hill | Bailey, Mt | 2.0 | 200 | Bailey |

### PLATTE RIVER MOUNTAINS–SORTED BY SUMMIT NAME

| Rank | Elev. | Summit Name | Parent | Mile | Rise | Quadrangle |
|------|-------|-------------|--------|------|------|------------|
|  | 12,303 | Blaine, Mt | South Twin Cone Pk | 1.0 | 203 | Mt Logan |
|  | 11,871 | Foster BM | South Twin Cone Pk | 1.4 | 211 | Mt Logan |
|  | 8,220 | Insmont Hill | Bailey, Mt | 2.0 | 200 | Bailey |
| 7 | 10,657 | Lost Platte Pk | Point 11,271 | 3.1 | 767 | Windy Pk |
|  | 9,300 | Mud Hill | Point 9,928 | 1.7 | 80 | Observatory Rock |
| 5 | 11,789 | No Payne | Shawnee Pk | 1.9 | 369 | Shawnee |
| 2 | 12,323 | North Twin Cone Pk | South Twin Cone Pk | 1.4 | 383 | Mt Logan |
| 6 | 11,780 | Payne BM | No Payne | 1.5 | 520 | Topaz Mtn |
| 3 | 11,941 | Platte Pk | Kenosha Pk | 1.3 | 401 | Shawnee |
| 8 | 10,190 | Point 10,190 | South Twin Cone Pk | 4.4 | 307 | Observatory Rock |
| 4 | 11,927 | Shawnee Pk | Platte Pk | 1.3 | 307 | Shawnee |
| 1 | 12,340 | South Twin Cone Pk | Pk X | 5.2 | 720 | Mt Logan |

# Colorado's Kenosha Mountains
## KENOSHA MOUNTAINS–SORTED BY ELEVATION

| Rank | Elev. | Summit Name | Parent | Mile | Rise | Quadrangle |
|---|---|---|---|---|---|---|
| 1 | 12,429 | Pk X | Logan, Mt | 9.0 | 1,749 | Topaz Mtn |
| 2 | 12,274 | Pk Y | Pk X | 1.0 | 534 | Topaz Mtn |
| 3 | 12,244 | Pk Z | Pk Y | 0.7 | 304 | Topaz Mtn |
| 4 | 12,100 | Kenosha Pk | South Twin Cone Pk | 2.4 | 320 | Mt Logan |
| S | 12,100 | X Prime | Pk X | 0.7 | 280 | Topaz Mtn |
| 5 | 12,067 | Zephyr | Pk Z | 1.0 | 337 | Topaz Mtn |
| 6 | 11,970 | Windy Pk | Bison Pk | 5.4 | 1,510 | Windy Pk |
| 7 | 11,589 | Buffalo Pk | Windy Pk | 4.2 | 929 | Green Mtn |
| 8 | 11,271 | Point 11,271 | Windy Pk | 3.4 | 484 | Windy Pk |
| 9 | 11,270 | Point 11,270 | Point 11,391 | 1.4 | 370 | Topaz Mtn |
| 10 | 11,230 | Point 11,230 | Windy Pk | 2.7 | 1,090 | Windy Pk |
| 11 | 11,180 | Point 11,180 A | Point 11,230 | 1.3 | 400 | Windy Pk |
| 12 | 11,060 | Point 11,060 | Point 11,271 | 2.1 | 579 | Topaz Mtn |
| 13 | 10,926 | Point 10,926 | Point 11,230 | 0.6 | 306 | Windy Pk |
| 14 | 10,654 | Point 10,654 | Point 11,180 A | 2.9 | 634 | McCurdy Mtn |
| 15 | 10,620 | Point 10,620 | Point 11,180 A | 1.0 | 560 | Windy Pk |
| 16 | 10,605 | Point 10,605 | Point 10,654 | 1.2 | 305 | McCurdy Mtn |
| 17 | 10,421 | Green Mtn | Buffalo Pk | 4.2 | 1,859 | Green Mtn |
| 18 | 9,691 | Castle, The | Buffalo Pk | 2.5 | 591 | Windy Pk |
| 19 | 9,500 | Point 9,500 | Buffalo Pk | 1.5 | 400 | Green Mtn |
| 20 | 9,242 | Point 9,242 | Point 9,300 | 0.7 | 342 | McCurdy Mtn |
| 21 | 9,192 | Little Scraggy Pk | Green Mtn | 1.5 | 772 | Green Mtn |
| 22 | 8,812 | Long Scraggy Pk | Little Scraggy Pk | 4.6 | 1,272 | Deckers |
| 23 | 8,783 | Redskin Mtn | Castle, The | 3.4 | 783 | Green Mtn |
| 24 | 8,722 | Point 8,722 | Redskin Mtn | 3.2 | 734 | Bailey |
| 25 | 8,685 | Point 8,685 | Point 9,500 | 2.0 | 465 | Cheesman Lake |
| 26 | 8,660 | Point 8,660 | Redskin Mtn | 1.7 | 440 | Windy Pk |
| 27 | 8,659 | Point 8,659 | Point 8,722 | 1.4 | 479 | Windy Pk |
| 28 | 8,501 | Sugarloaf Pk | Point 8,685 | 0.9 | 561 | Cheesman Lake |
| 29 | 8,494 | Point 8,494 | Castle, The | 1.1 | 474 | Green Mtn |
| 30 | 8,484 | Point 8,484 | Point 8,660 | 0.6 | 344 | Green Mtn |
| S | 8,260 | Point 8,260 | Point 8,659 | 0.8 | 280 | Bailey |
| S | 8,232 | Point 8,232 | Sugarloaf Pk | 0.4 | 292 | Green Mtn |
| 31 | 8,183 | Raleigh Pk | Cathedral Spires | 2.9 | 643 | Platte Canyon |
| 32 | 8,140 | Point 8,140 | Redskin Mtn | 2.7 | 400 | Pine |
| 33 | 8,020 | Chair Rocks | Raleigh Pk | 1.4 | 320 | Platte Canyon |
| 34 | 7,980 | Point 7,980 | Point 8,140 | 1.4 | 440 | Pine |
| 35 | 7,933 | Cheesman Mtn | Sugarloaf Pk | 1.2 | 753 | Cheesman Lake |

## KENOSHA MOUNTAINS–SORTED BY ELEVATION *(continued)*

| Rank | Elev. | Summit Name | Parent | Mile | Rise | Quadrangle |
|---|---|---|---|---|---|---|
| 36 | 7,872 | Baldy Pk | Point 8,140 | 1.3 | 332 | Green Mtn |
| | 7,822 | Wigwam BM | Point 8,685 | 1.9 | 2 | Cheesman Lake |
| | 7,180 | Skull Rock | Cheesman Mtn | 2.8 | 240 | Deckers |
| | 6,460 | Eagle Rock | Bennett Mtn | 2.2 | 120 | Platte Canyon |

## KENOSHA MOUNTAINS–SORTED BY SUMMIT NAME

| Rank | Elev. | Summit Name | Parent | Mile | Rise | Quadrangle |
|---|---|---|---|---|---|---|
| 36 | 7,872 | Baldy Pk | Point 8,140 | 1.3 | 332 | Green Mtn |
| 7 | 11,589 | Buffalo Pk | Windy Pk | 4.2 | 929 | Green Mtn |
| 18 | 9,691 | Castle, The | Buffalo Pk | 2.5 | 591 | Windy Pk |
| 33 | 8,020 | Chair Rocks | Raleigh Pk | 1.4 | 320 | Platte Canyon |
| 35 | 7,933 | Cheesman Mtn | Sugarloaf Pk | 1.2 | 753 | Cheesman Lake |
| | 6,460 | Eagle Rock | Bennett Mtn | 2.2 | 120 | Platte Canyon |
| 17 | 10,421 | Green Mtn | Buffalo Pk | 4.2 | 1,859 | Green Mtn |
| 4 | 12,100 | Kenosha Pk | South Twin Cone Pk | 2.4 | 320 | Mt Logan |
| 21 | 9,192 | Little Scraggy Pk | Green Mtn | 1.5 | 772 | Green Mtn |
| 22 | 8,812 | Long Scraggy Pk | Little Scraggy Pk | 4.6 | 1,272 | Deckers |
| 1 | 12,429 | Pk X | Logan, Mt | 9.0 | 1,749 | Topaz Mtn |
| 2 | 12,274 | Pk Y | Pk X | 1.0 | 534 | Topaz Mtn |
| 3 | 12,244 | Pk Z | Pk Y | 0.7 | 304 | Topaz Mtn |
| 8 | 11,271 | Point 11,271 | Windy Pk | 3.4 | 484 | Windy Pk |
| 9 | 11,270 | Point 11,270 | Point 11,391 | 1.4 | 370 | Topaz Mtn |
| 10 | 11,230 | Point 11,230 | Windy Pk | 2.7 | 1,090 | Windy Pk |
| 11 | 11,180 | Point 11,180 A | Point 11,230 | 1.3 | 400 | Windy Pk |
| 12 | 11,060 | Point 11,060 | Point 11,271 | 2.1 | 579 | Topaz Mtn |
| 13 | 10,926 | Point 10,926 | Point 11,230 | 0.6 | 306 | Windy Pk |
| 14 | 10,654 | Point 10,654 | Point 11,180 A | 2.9 | 634 | McCurdy Mtn |
| 15 | 10,620 | Point 10,620 | Point 11,180 A | 1.0 | 560 | Windy Pk |
| 16 | 10,605 | Point 10,605 | Point 10,654 | 1.2 | 305 | McCurdy Mtn |
| 19 | 9,500 | Point 9,500 | Buffalo Pk | 1.5 | 400 | Green Mtn |
| 20 | 9,242 | Point 9,242 | Point 9,300 | 0.7 | 342 | McCurdy Mtn |
| 24 | 8,722 | Point 8,722 | Redskin Mtn | 3.2 | 734 | Bailey |
| 25 | 8,685 | Point 8,685 | Point 9,500 | 2.0 | 465 | Cheesman Lake |
| 26 | 8,660 | Point 8,660 | Redskin Mtn | 1.7 | 440 | Windy Pk |
| 27 | 8,659 | Point 8,659 | Point 8,722 | 1.4 | 479 | Windy Pk |
| 29 | 8,494 | Point 8,494 | Castle, The | 1.1 | 474 | Green Mtn |
| 30 | 8,484 | Point 8,484 | Point 8,660 | 0.6 | 344 | Green Mtn |
| S | 8,260 | Point 8,260 | Point 8,659 | 0.8 | 280 | Bailey |
| S | 8,232 | Point 8,232 | Sugarloaf Pk | 0.4 | 292 | Green Mtn |
| 32 | 8,140 | Point 8,140 | Redskin Mtn | 2.7 | 400 | Pine |

| Rank | Elev. | Summit Name | Parent | Mile | Rise | Quadrangle |
|------|-------|-------------|--------|------|------|------------|
| 34 | 7,980 | Point 7,980 | Point 8,140 | 1.4 | 440 | Pine |
| 31 | 8,183 | Raleigh Pk | Cathedral Spires | 2.9 | 643 | Platte Canyon |
| 23 | 8,783 | Redskin Mtn | Castle, The | 3.4 | 783 | Green Mtn |
| | 7,180 | Skull Rock | Cheesman Mtn | 2.8 | 240 | Deckers |
| 28 | 8,501 | Sugarloaf Pk | Point 8,685 | 0.9 | 561 | Cheesman Lake |
| | 7,822 | Wigwam BM | Point 8,685 | 1.9 | 2 | Cheesman Lake |
| 6 | 11,970 | Windy Pk | Bison Pk | 5.4 | 1,510 | Windy Pk |
| S | 12,100 | X Prime | Pk X | 0.7 | 280 | Topaz Mtn |
| 5 | 12,067 | Zephyr | Pk Z | 1.0 | 337 | Topaz Mtn |

115

# Colorado's Tarryall Mountains

## Tarryall Mountains–Sorted by Elevation

| Rank | Elev. | Summit Name | Parent | Mile | Rise | Quadrangle |
|------|-------|-------------|--------|------|------|------------|
| 1 | 12,431 | Bison Pk | Logan, Mt | 19.2 | 2,451 | McCurdy Mtn |
| 2 | 12,168 | McCurdy Mtn | Bison Pk | 2.1 | 789 | McCurdy Mtn |
| 3 | 11,902 | North Tarryall Pk | Pk Z | 3.4 | 872 | Topaz Mtn |
| 4 | 11,780 | Tarryall Pk | McCurdy Mtn | 2.7 | 920 | McCurdy Mtn |
| 5 | 11,762 | Point 11,762 | McCurdy Mtn | 1.1 | 342 | McCurdy Mtn |
| 6 | 11,762 | Topaz Mtn | North Tarryall Pk | 2.4 | 662 | Topaz Mtn |
| 7 | 11,611 | Point 11,611 | Topaz Mtn | 2.6 | 391 | Topaz Mtn |
| 8 | 11,469 | Point 11,469 | Point 11,611 | 1.6 | 329 | Farnum Pk |
| 9 | 11,460 | Point 11,460 | Point 11,762 | 1.0 | 560 | McCurdy Mtn |
| 10 | 11,423 | Point 11,423 | Point 11,469 | 1.8 | 603 | Topaz Mtn |
| 11 | 11,403 | Lake Park Pk | Tarryall Pk | 1.0 | 503 | McCurdy Mtn |
| 12 | 11,391 | Point 11,391 | North Tarryall Pk | 1.5 | 371 | Topaz Mtn |
| 13 | 11,328 | Point 11,328 | Point 11,460 | 0.9 | 468 | McCurdy Mtn |
| 14 | 11,306 | Point 11,306 | Point 11,611 | 1.3 | 326 | Topaz Mtn |
| 15 | 11,206 | South Tarryall Pk | Lake Park Pk | 1.7 | 1,186 | McCurdy Mtn |
| 16 | 11,180 | Point 11,180 B | McCurdy Mtn | 1.2 | 360 | McCurdy Mtn |
| 17 | 10,982 | Point 10,982 | South Tarryall Pk | 2.5 | 482 | McCurdy Mtn |
| S | 10,624 | Pilot Pk | Point 10,982 | 1.2 | 284 | Tarryall |
| S | 10,624 | Point 10,624 | Point 11,391 | 1.6 | 284 | Observatory Rock |
| 18 | 9,951 | Sugarloaf Mtn | Point 11,611 | 2.4 | 467 | Farnum Pk |
| | 9,940 | X Rock | Point 11,762 | 1.1 | 120 | McCurdy Mtn |
| 19 | 9,489 | Bradley Pk | Point 10,462 | 2.5 | 495 | McCurdy Mtn |
| | 9,310 | Al Hill | Eagle Rock | 1.8 | 177 | Eagle Rock |
| 20 | 9,300 | Point 9,300 | Point 11,328 | 1.4 | 360 | McCurdy Mtn |
| | 9,236 | Reese BM | Eagle Rock | 2.7 | 56 | Observatory Rock |
| | 9,193 | Rob BM | Point 9,870 | 1.6 | 13 | Observatory Rock |

## TARRYALL MOUNTAINS–SORTED BY ELEVATION *(continued)*

| Rank | Elev. | Summit Name | Parent | Mile | Rise | Quadrangle |
|---|---|---|---|---|---|---|
| 21 | 9,111 | Point 9,111 | China Wall | 1.3 | 331 | McCurdy Mtn |
| 22 | 8,906 | Point 8,906 | Tappan Mtn | 1.0 | 326 | Tarryall |
| 23 | 8,877 | North Sheeprock | Point 10,654 | 3.4 | 977 | Cheesman Lake |
| 24 | 8,740 | South Sheeprock | North Sheeprock | 1.7 | 520 | Cheesman Lake |
| 25 | 8,671 | East Sheeprock | South Sheeprock | 0.7 | 451 | Cheesman Lake |
| S | 8,220 | Point 8,220 | Point 8,285 | 0.5 | 280 | Cheesman Lake |

## TARRYALL MOUNTAINS–SORTED BY SUMMIT NAME

| Rank | Elev. | Summit Name | Parent | Mile | Rise | Quadrangle |
|---|---|---|---|---|---|---|
|  | 9,310 | Al Hill | Eagle Rock | 1.8 | 177 | Eagle Rock |
| 1 | 12,431 | Bison Pk | Logan, Mt | 19.2 | 2,451 | McCurdy Mtn |
| 19 | 9,489 | Bradley Pk | Point 10,462 | 2.5 | 495 | McCurdy Mtn |
| 25 | 8,671 | East Sheeprock | South Sheeprock | 0.7 | 451 | Cheesman Lake |
| 11 | 11,403 | Lake Park Pk | Tarryall Pk | 1.0 | 503 | McCurdy Mtn |
| 2 | 12,168 | McCurdy Mtn | Bison Pk | 2.1 | 789 | McCurdy Mtn |
| 23 | 8,877 | North Sheeprock | Point 10,654 | 3.4 | 977 | Cheesman Lake |
| 3 | 11,902 | North Tarryall Pk | Pk Z | 3.4 | 872 | Topaz Mtn |
| S | 10,624 | Pilot Pk | Point 10,982 | 1.2 | 284 | Tarryall |
| 5 | 11,762 | Point 11,762 | McCurdy Mtn | 1.1 | 342 | McCurdy Mtn |
| 7 | 11,611 | Point 11,611 | Topaz Mtn | 2.6 | 391 | Topaz Mtn |
| 8 | 11,469 | Point 11,469 | Point 11,611 | 1.6 | 329 | Farnum Pk |
| 9 | 11,460 | Point 11,460 | Point 11,762 | 1.0 | 560 | McCurdy Mtn |
| 10 | 11,423 | Point 11,423 | Point 11,469 | 1.8 | 603 | Topaz Mtn |
| 12 | 11,391 | Point 11,391 | North Tarryall Pk | 1.5 | 371 | Topaz Mtn |
| 13 | 11,328 | Point 11,328 | Point 11,460 | 0.9 | 468 | McCurdy Mtn |
| 14 | 11,306 | Point 11,306 | Point 11,611 | 1.3 | 326 | Topaz Mtn |
| 16 | 11,180 | Point 11,180 B | McCurdy Mtn | 1.2 | 360 | McCurdy Mtn |
| 17 | 10,982 | Point 10,982 | South Tarryall Pk | 2.5 | 482 | McCurdy Mtn |
| S | 10,624 | Point 10,624 | Point 11,391 | 1.6 | 284 | Observatory Rock |
| 20 | 9,300 | Point 9,300 | Point 11,328 | 1.4 | 360 | McCurdy Mtn |
| 21 | 9,111 | Point 9,111 | China Wall | 1.3 | 331 | McCurdy Mtn |
| 22 | 8,906 | Point 8,906 | Tappan Mtn | 1.0 | 326 | Tarryall |
| S | 8,220 | Point 8,220 | Point 8,285 | 0.5 | 280 | Cheesman Lake |
|  | 9,236 | Reese BM | Eagle Rock | 2.7 | 56 | Observatory Rock |
|  | 9,193 | Rob BM | Point 9,870 | 1.6 | 13 | Observatory Rock |
| 24 | 8,740 | South Sheeprock | North Sheeprock | 1.7 | 520 | Cheesman Lake |
| 15 | 11,206 | South Tarryall Pk | Point 11,403 | 1.7 | 1,186 | McCurdy Mtn |
| 18 | 9,951 | Sugarloaf Mtn | Point 11,611 | 2.4 | 467 | Farnum Pk |
| 4 | 11,780 | Tarryall Pk | McCurdy Mtn | 2.7 | 920 | McCurdy Mtn |

| Rank | Elev. | Summit Name | Parent | Mile | Rise | Quadrangle |
|------|-------|-------------|--------|------|------|------------|
| 6 | 11,762 | Topaz Mtn | North Tarryall Pk | 2.4 | 662 | Topaz Mtn |
|  | 9,940 | X Rock | Point 11,762 | 1.1 | 120 | McCurdy Mtn |

# Colorado's Puma Hills

## Puma Hills–Sorted by Elevation

| Rank | Elev. | Summit Name | Parent | Mile | Rise | Quadrangle |
|------|-------|-------------|--------|------|------|------------|
| 1 | 11,570 | Puma Pk | Point 11,762 | 7.3 | 2,240 | Farnum Pk |
| 2 | 11,449 | Little Puma | Puma Pk | 1.1 | 495 | Farnum Pk |
|  | 11,377 | Farnum Pk | Little Puma | 0.6 | 277 | Farnum Pk |
| 3 | 11,332 | Schoolmarm Mtn | Puma Pk | 2.7 | 632 | Glentivar |
| 4 | 11,294 | Badger Mtn | Schoolmarm Mtn | 6.3 | 1,594 | Glentivar |
| 5 | 11,289 | Martland Pk | Schoolmarm Mtn | 1.5 | 463 | Glentivar |
| 6 | 11,085 | Burntop | Little Puma | 1.8 | 505 | Farnum Pk |
| 7 | 11,053 | Point 11,053 | Badger Mtn | 0.8 | 313 | Glentivar |
| 8 | 10,879 | Stoll Mtn | Badger Pk | 4.0 | 1,379 | Spinney Mtn |
| 9 | 10,868 | Point 10,868 | Martland Pk | 2.3 | 848 | Farnum Pk |
| 10 | 10,721 | Point 10,721 | Schoolmarm Mtn | 1.4 | 341 | Farnum Pk |
| 11 | 10,715 | Point 10,715 | Martland Pk | 0.8 | 453 | Glentivar |
| 12 | 10,568 | Point 10,568 | Point 11,053 | 1.2 | 308 | Glentivar |
| 13 | 10,558 | Reinecker Ridge | Little Baldy Mtn | 7.8 | 811 | Fairplay East |
| 14 | 10,538 | Pulver Mtn | Stoll Mtn | 1.6 | 318 | Glentivar |
| 15 | 10,462 | Point 10,462 | Point 10,868 | 1.6 | 678 | Farnum Pk |
|  | 10,460 | Rishaberger Mtn | Schoolmarm Mtn | 1.3 | 240 | Glentivar |
| 16 | 10,412 | Roachaburger | Schoolmarm Mtn | 2.0 | 392 | Sulphur Mtn |
| 17 | 10,380 | Point 10,380 | Pulver Mtn | 0.9 | 560 | Glentivar |
| 18 | 10,378 | Point 10,378 | Point 10,715 | 0.6 | 301 | Glentivar |
| 19 | 10,368 | Indian BM | Burntop | 8.9 | 1,038 | Eagle Rock |
|  | 10,363 | Basin2 BM | Reinecker Ridge | 2.5 | 113 | Fairplay East |
| 20 | 10,341 | Point 10,341 | Reinecker Ridge | 3.1 | 355 | Fairplay East |
| 21 | 10,340 | Point 10,340 | Stoll Mtn | 1.6 | 440 | Elevenmile Canyon |
| S | 10,300 | Point 10,300 | Puma Pk | 1.3 | 280 | Farnum Pk |
| 22 | 10,289 | Point 10,289 | Indian BM | 1.2 | 399 | Eagle Rock |
| 23 | 10,274 | Point 10,274 | Reinecker Ridge | 1.4 | 344 | Fairplay East |
| 24 | 10,207 | Point 10,207 | Point 10,715 | 0.9 | 347 | Glentivar |
| 25 | 10,122 | Mexican Ridge | Point 10,274 | 1.4 | 612 | Elkhorn |
| 26 | 10,093 | Point 10,093 | Point 10,378 | 0.5 | 313 | Glentivar |
| 27 | 10,073 | Observatory Rock | Indian BM | 2.7 | 573 | Observatory Rock |
| 28 | 10,069 | Point 10,069 | Point 10,380 | 1.2 | 649 | Glentivar |

## Puma Hills–Sorted by Elevation *(continued)*

| Rank | Elev. | Summit Name | Parent | Mile | Rise | Quadrangle |
|------|-------|-------------|--------|------|------|------------|
| S | 10,060 | Point 10,060 | Roachaburger | 1.3 | 291 | Glentivar |
| 29 | 10,030 | Point 10,030 | Indian BM | 3.0 | 340 | Elkhorn |
| 30 | 9,986 | Point 9,986 | Point 10,030 | 5.9 | 356 | Elkhorn |
| 31 | 9,928 | Point 9,928 | Indian BM | 2.5 | 388 | Observatory Rock |
|  | 9,921 | Elkhorn BM | Point 9,986 | 1.4 | 271 | Elkhorn |
| 32 | 9,900 | Point 9,900 | Point 10,340 | 2.7 | 840 | Elevenmile Canyon |
| 33 | 9,898 | Mania BM | Point 9,986 | 4.2 | 508 | Sulphur Mtn |
| 34 | 9,895 | Point 9,895 | Burntop | 2.3 | 355 | Eagle Rock |
| 35 | 9,870 | Point 9,870 | Observatory Rock | 1.1 | 330 | Observatory Rock |
| 36 | 9,833 | Point 9,833 | Point 9,986 | 2.0 | 303 | Sulphur Mtn |
|  | 9,830 | Logan Hill | Point 9,986 | 1.0 | 180 | Elkhorn |
| 37 | 9,752 | Point 9,752 | Point 10,868 | 2.4 | 452 | Glentivar |
|  | 9,726 | Clark BM | Mexican Ridge | 1.8 | 106 | Milligan Lakes |
| 38 | 9,710 | Eagle Rock | Point 9,895 | 2.9 | 500 | Eagle Rock |
| 39 | 9,706 | Point 9,706 | Badger Mtn | 1.6 | 326 | Tarryall |
| 40 | 9,556 | Bald Hill | Point 9,619 | 4.1 | 466 | Hartsel |
|  | 9,544 | Baker Mtn | Point 10,289 | 2.2 | 154 | Eagle Rock |
|  | 9,528 | Link Spring Ridge | Point 10,030 | 2.0 | 98 | Elkhorn |
| 41 | 9,524 | Spinney Mtn | Point 10,069 | 4.0 | 814 | Spinney Mtn |
| S | 9,422 | Point 9,422 | Point 9,900 | 1.0 | 282 | Elevenmile Canyon |
| 42 | 9,380 | Point 9,380 A | Bradley Pk | 1.3 | 320 | McCurdy Mtn |
| 43 | 9,380 | Point 9,380 B | Pulver Mtn | 1.9 | 320 | Tarryall |
| 44 | 9,339 | Sulphur Mtn | Roachaburger | 4.7 | 529 | Sulphur Mtn |
| 45 | 9,241 | Point 9,241 | Point 9,900 | 1.6 | 381 | Elevenmile Canyon |
| S | 9,220 | Point 9,220 | Point 9,422 | 0.9 | 280 | Elevenmile Canyon |
| 46 | 9,189 | China Wall | Point 9,752 | 2.6 | 409 | Tarryall |
| 47 | 9,162 | Point 9,162 | Point 9,241 | 1.5 | 422 | Elevenmile Canyon |
| 48 | 9,137 | Point 9,137 | Point 9,162 | 2.3 | 317 | Tarryall |
| 49 | 9,083 | Point 9,083 | Point 9,137 | 4.5 | 783 | Hackett Mtn |
| 50 | 9,036 | Point 9,036 | Point 9,083 | 2.5 | 536 | Hackett Mtn |
| S | 9,033 | Round Mtn | Point 9,706 | 2.4 | 293 | Tarryall |
| S | 9,020 | Point 9,020 | Point 9,900 | 1.9 | 280 | Elevenmile Canyon |
| 51 | 8,980 | Point 8,980 | Point 9,162 | 1.9 | 360 | Elevenmile Canyon |
| 52 | 8,954 | Tappan Mtn | Point 9,036 | 1.7 | 534 | Tarryall |
| 53 | 8,729 | Point 8,729 | Point 9,162 | 1.1 | 309 | Elevenmile Canyon |

## Puma Hills–Sorted by Summit Name

| Rank | Elev. | Summit Name | Parent | Mile | Rise | Quadrangle |
|------|-------|-------------|--------|------|------|------------|
| 4 | 11,294 | Badger Mtn | Schoolmarm Mtn | 6.3 | 1,594 | Glentivar |
|  | 9,544 | Baker Mtn | Point 10,289 | 2.2 | 154 | Eagle Rock |

## PUMA HILLS–SORTED BY SUMMIT NAME *(continued)*

| Rank | Elev. | Summit Name | Parent | Mile | Rise | Quadrangle |
|------|-------|-------------|--------|------|------|------------|
| 40 | 9,556 | Bald Hill | Point 9,619 | 4.1 | 466 | Hartsel |
| | 10,363 | Basin2 BM | Reinecker Ridge | 2.5 | 113 | Fairplay East |
| 6 | 11,085 | Burntop | Little Puma | 1.8 | 505 | Farnum Pk |
| 46 | 9,189 | China Wall | Point 9,752 | 2.6 | 409 | Tarryall |
| | 9,726 | Clark BM | Mexican Ridge | 1.8 | 106 | Milligan Lakes |
| 38 | 9,710 | Eagle Rock | Point 9,895 | 2.9 | 500 | Eagle Rock |
| | 9,921 | Elkhorn BM | Point 9,986 | 1.4 | 271 | Elkhorn |
| | 11,377 | Farnum Pk | Little Puma | 0.6 | 277 | Farnum Pk |
| 19 | 10,368 | Indian BM | Burntop | 8.9 | 1,038 | Eagle Rock |
| | 9,528 | Link Spring Ridge | Point 10,030 | 2.0 | 98 | Elkhorn |
| 2 | 11,449 | Little Puma | Puma Pk | 1.1 | 495 | Farnum Pk |
| | 9,830 | Logan Hill | Point 9,986 | 1.0 | 180 | Elkhorn |
| 33 | 9,898 | Mania BM | Point 9,986 | 4.2 | 508 | Sulphur Mtn |
| 5 | 11,289 | Martland Pk | Schoolmarm Mtn | 1.5 | 463 | Glentivar |
| 25 | 10,122 | Mexican Ridge | Point 10,274 | 1.4 | 612 | Elkhorn |
| 27 | 10,073 | Observatory Rock | Indian BM | 2.7 | 573 | Observatory Rock |
| 7 | 11,053 | Point 11,053 | Badger Mtn | 0.8 | 313 | Glentivar |
| 9 | 10,868 | Point 10,868 | Martland Pk | 2.3 | 848 | Farnum Pk |
| 10 | 10,721 | Point 10,721 | Schoolmarm Mtn | 1.4 | 341 | Farnum Pk |
| 11 | 10,715 | Point 10,715 | Martland Pk | 0.8 | 453 | Glentivar |
| 12 | 10,568 | Point 10,568 | Point 11,053 | 1.2 | 308 | Glentivar |
| 15 | 10,462 | Point 10,462 | Point 10,868 | 1.6 | 678 | Farnum Pk |
| 17 | 10,380 | Point 10,380 | Pulver Mtn | 0.9 | 560 | Glentivar |
| 18 | 10,378 | Point 10,378 | Point 10,715 | 0.6 | 301 | Glentivar |
| 20 | 10,341 | Point 10,341 | Reinecker Ridge | 3.1 | 355 | Fairplay East |
| 21 | 10,340 | Point 10,340 | Stoll Mtn | 1.6 | 440 | Elevenmile Canyon |
| S | 10,300 | Point 10,300 | Puma Pk | 1.3 | 280 | Farnum Pk |
| 22 | 10,289 | Point 10,289 | Indian BM | 1.2 | 399 | Eagle Rock |
| 23 | 10,274 | Point 10,274 | Reinecker Ridge | 1.4 | 344 | Fairplay East |
| 24 | 10,207 | Point 10,207 | Point 10,715 | 0.9 | 347 | Glentivar |
| 26 | 10,093 | Point 10,093 | Point 10,378 | 0.5 | 313 | Glentivar |
| 28 | 10,069 | Point 10,069 | Point 10,380 | 1.2 | 649 | Glentivar |
| S | 10,060 | Point 10,060 | Roachaburger | 1.3 | 291 | Glentivar |
| 29 | 10,030 | Point 10,030 | Indian BM | 3.0 | 340 | Elkhorn |
| 30 | 9,986 | Point 9,986 | Point 10,030 | 5.9 | 356 | Elkhorn |
| 31 | 9,928 | Point 9,928 | Indian BM | 2.5 | 388 | Observatory Rock |
| 32 | 9,900 | Point 9,900 | Point 10,340 | 2.7 | 840 | Elevenmile Canyon |
| 34 | 9,895 | Point 9,895 | Burntop | 2.3 | 355 | Eagle Rock |
| 35 | 9,870 | Point 9,870 | Observatory Rock | 1.1 | 330 | Observatory Rock |
| 36 | 9,833 | Point 9,833 | Point 9,986 | 2.0 | 303 | Sulphur Mtn |

## Puma Hills–Sorted by Summit Name *(continued)*

| Rank | Elev. | Summit Name | Parent | Mile | Rise | Quadrangle |
|---|---|---|---|---|---|---|
| 37 | 9,752 | Point 9,752 | Point 10,868 | 2.4 | 452 | Glentivar |
| 39 | 9,706 | Point 9,706 | Badger Mtn | 1.6 | 326 | Tarryall |
| S | 9,422 | Point 9,422 | Point 9,900 | 1.0 | 282 | Elevenmile Canyon |
| 42 | 9,380 | Point 9,380 A | Bradley Pk | 1.3 | 320 | McCurdy Mtn |
| 43 | 9,380 | Point 9,380 B | Pulver Mtn | 1.9 | 320 | Tarryall |
| 45 | 9,241 | Point 9,241 | Point 9,900 | 1.6 | 381 | Elevenmile Canyon |
| S | 9,220 | Point 9,220 | Point 9,422 | 0.9 | 280 | Elevenmile Canyon |
| 47 | 9,162 | Point 9,162 | Point 9,241 | 1.5 | 422 | Elevenmile Canyon |
| 48 | 9,137 | Point 9,137 | Point 9,162 | 2.3 | 317 | Tarryall |
| 49 | 9,083 | Point 9,083 | Point 9,137 | 4.5 | 783 | Hackett Mtn |
| 50 | 9,036 | Point 9,036 | Point 9,083 | 2.5 | 536 | Hackett Mtn |
| S | 9,020 | Point 9,020 | Point 9,900 | 1.9 | 280 | Elevenmile Canyon |
| 51 | 8,980 | Point 8,980 | Point 9,162 | 1.9 | 360 | Elevenmile Canyon |
| 53 | 8,729 | Point 8,729 | Point 9,162 | 1.1 | 309 | Elevenmile Canyon |
| 14 | 10,538 | Pulver Mtn | Stoll Mtn | 1.6 | 318 | Glentivar |
| 1 | 11,570 | Puma Pk | Point 11,762 | 7.3 | 2,240 | Farnum Pk |
| 13 | 10,558 | Reinecker Ridge | Little Baldy Mtn | 7.8 | 811 | Fairplay East |
|  | 10,460 | Rishaberger Mtn | Schoolmarm Mtn | 1.3 | 240 | Glentivar |
| 16 | 10,412 | Roachaburger | Schoolmarm Mtn | 2.0 | 392 | Sulphur Mtn |
| S | 9,033 | Round Mtn | Point 9,706 | 2.4 | 293 | Tarryall |
| 3 | 11,332 | Schoolmarm Mtn | Puma Pk | 2.7 | 632 | Glentivar |
| 41 | 9,524 | Spinney Mtn | Point 10,069 | 4.0 | 814 | Spinney Mtn |
| 8 | 10,879 | Stoll Mtn | Badger Pk | 4.0 | 1,379 | Spinney Mtn |
| 44 | 9,339 | Sulphur Mtn | Roachaburger | 4.7 | 529 | Sulphur Mtn |
| 52 | 8,954 | Tappan Mtn | Point 9,036 | 1.7 | 534 | Tarryall |

# Colorado's Retirement Range
## Retirement Range–Sorted by Elevation

| Rank | Elev. | Summit Name | Parent | Mile | Rise | Quadrangle |
|---|---|---|---|---|---|---|
| 1 | 12,431 | Bison Pk | Logan, Mt | 19.2 | 2,451 | McCurdy Mtn |
| 2 | 12,429 | Pk X | Logan, Mt | 9.0 | 1,749 | Topaz Mtn |
| 3 | 12,340 | South Twin Cone Pk | Pk X | 5.2 | 720 | Mt Logan |
| 4 | 12,323 | North Twin Cone Pk | South Twin Cone Pk | 1.4 | 383 | Mt Logan |
|  | 12,303 | Blaine, Mt | South Twin Cone Pk | 1.0 | 203 | Mt Logan |
| 5 | 12,274 | Pk Y | Pk X | 1.0 | 534 | Topaz Mtn |
| 6 | 12,244 | Pk Z | Pk Y | 0.7 | 304 | Topaz Mtn |
| 7 | 12,168 | McCurdy Mtn | Bison Pk | 2.1 | 789 | McCurdy Mtn |
| 8 | 12,100 | Kenosha Pk | South Twin Cone Pk | 2.4 | 320 | Mt Logan |
| S | 12,100 | X Prime | Pk X | 0.7 | 280 | Topaz Mtn |

### RETIREMENT RANGE–SORTED BY ELEVATION *(continued)*

| Rank | Elev. | Summit Name | Parent | Mile | Rise | Quadrangle |
|------|-------|-------------|--------|------|------|------------|
| 9 | 12,067 | Zephyr | Pk Z | 1.0 | 337 | Topaz Mtn |
| 10 | 11,970 | Windy Pk | Bison Pk | 5.4 | 1,510 | Windy Pk |
| 11 | 11,941 | Platte Pk | Kenosha Pk | 1.3 | 401 | Shawnee |
| 12 | 11,927 | Shawnee Pk | Platte Pk | 1.3 | 307 | Shawnee |
| 13 | 11,902 | North Tarryall Pk | Pk Z | 3.4 | 872 | Topaz Mtn |
| | 11,871 | Foster BM | South Twin Cone Pk | 1.4 | 211 | Mt Logan |
| 14 | 11,789 | No Payne | Shawnee Pk | 1.9 | 369 | Shawnee |
| 15 | 11,780 | Payne BM | No Payne | 1.5 | 520 | Topaz Mtn |
| 16 | 11,780 | Tarryall Pk | McCurdy Mtn | 2.7 | 920 | McCurdy Mtn |
| 17 | 11,762 | Point 11,762 | McCurdy Mtn | 1.1 | 342 | McCurdy Mtn |
| 18 | 11,762 | Topaz Mtn | North Tarryall Pk | 2.4 | 662 | Topaz Mtn |
| 19 | 11,611 | Point 11,611 | Topaz Mtn | 2.6 | 391 | Topaz Mtn |
| 20 | 11,589 | Buffalo Pk | Windy Pk | 4.2 | 929 | Green Mtn |
| 21 | 11,570 | Puma Pk | Point 11,762 | 7.3 | 2,240 | Farnum Pk |
| 22 | 11,469 | Point 11,469 | Point 11,611 | 1.6 | 329 | Farnum Pk |
| 23 | 11,460 | Point 11,460 | Point 11,762 | 1.0 | 560 | McCurdy Mtn |
| 24 | 11,449 | Little Puma | Puma Pk | 1.1 | 495 | Farnum Pk |
| 25 | 11,423 | Point 11,423 | Point 11,469 | 1.8 | 603 | Topaz Mtn |
| 26 | 11,403 | Lake Park Pk | Tarryall Pk | 1.0 | 503 | McCurdy Mtn |
| 27 | 11,391 | Point 11,391 | North Tarryall Pk | 1.5 | 371 | Topaz Mtn |
| | 11,377 | Farnum Pk | Little Puma | 0.6 | 277 | Farnum Pk |
| 28 | 11,332 | Schoolmarm Mtn | Puma Pk | 2.7 | 632 | Glentivar |
| 29 | 11,328 | Point 11,328 | Point 11,460 | 0.9 | 468 | McCurdy Mtn |
| 30 | 11,306 | Point 11,306 | Point 11,611 | 1.3 | 326 | Topaz Mtn |
| 31 | 11,294 | Badger Mtn | Schoolmarm Mtn | 6.3 | 1,594 | Glentivar |
| 32 | 11,289 | Martland Pk | Schoolmarm Mtn | 1.5 | 463 | Glentivar |
| 33 | 11,271 | Point 11,271 | Windy Pk | 3.4 | 484 | Windy Pk |
| 34 | 11,270 | Point 11,270 | Point 11,391 | 1.4 | 370 | Topaz Mtn |
| 35 | 11,230 | Point 11,230 | Windy Pk | 2.7 | 1,090 | Windy Pk |
| 36 | 11,206 | South Tarryall Pk | Point 11,403 | 1.7 | 1,186 | McCurdy Mtn |
| 37 | 11,180 | Point 11,180 A | Point 11,230 | 1.3 | 400 | Windy Pk |
| 38 | 11,180 | Point 11,180 B | McCurdy Mtn | 1.2 | 360 | McCurdy Mtn |
| 39 | 11,085 | Burntop | Little Puma | 1.8 | 505 | Farnum Pk |
| 40 | 11,060 | Point 11,060 | Point 11,271 | 2.1 | 579 | Topaz Mtn |
| 41 | 11,053 | Point 11,053 | Badger Mtn | 0.8 | 313 | Glentivar |
| 42 | 10,982 | Point 10,982 | South Tarryall Pk | 2.5 | 482 | McCurdy Mtn |
| 43 | 10,926 | Point 10,926 | Point 11,230 | 0.6 | 306 | Windy Pk |
| 44 | 10,879 | Stoll Mtn | Badger Pk | 4.0 | 1,379 | Spinney Mtn |
| 45 | 10,868 | Point 10,868 | Martland Pk | 2.3 | 848 | Farnum Pk |
| 46 | 10,721 | Point 10,721 | Schoolmarm Mtn | 1.4 | 341 | Farnum Pk |

## Retirement Range–Sorted by Elevation *(continued)*

| Rank | Elev. | Summit Name | Parent | Mile | Rise | Quadrangle |
|------|-------|-------------|--------|------|------|------------|
| 47 | 10,715 | Point 10,715 | Martland Pk | 0.8 | 453 | Glentivar |
| 48 | 10,657 | Lost Platte Peak | Point 11,271 | 3.1 | 767 | Windy Pk |
| 49 | 10,654 | Point 10,654 | Point 11,180 A | 2.9 | 634 | McCurdy Mtn |
| S | 10,624 | Pilot Pk | Point 10,982 | 1.2 | 284 | Tarryall |
| S | 10,624 | Point 10,624 | Point 11,391 | 1.6 | 284 | Observatory Rock |
| 50 | 10,620 | Point 10,620 | Point 11,180 A | 1.0 | 560 | Windy Pk |
| 51 | 10,605 | Point 10,605 | Point 10,654 | 1.2 | 305 | McCurdy Mtn |
| 52 | 10,568 | Point 10,568 | Point 11,053 | 1.2 | 308 | Glentivar |
| 53 | 10,558 | Reinecker Ridge | Little Baldy Mtn | 7.8 | 811 | Fairplay East |
| 54 | 10,538 | Pulver Mtn | Stoll Mtn | 1.6 | 318 | Glentivar |
| 55 | 10,462 | Point 10,462 | Point 10,868 | 1.6 | 678 | Farnum Pk |
|  | 10,460 | Rishaberger Mtn | Schoolmarm Mtn | 1.3 | 240 | Glentivar |
| 56 | 10,421 | Green Mtn | Buffalo Pk | 4.2 | 1,859 | Green Mtn |
| 57 | 10,412 | Roachaburger | Schoolmarm Mtn | 2.0 | 392 | Sulphur Mtn |
| 58 | 10,380 | Point 10,380 | Pulver Mtn | 0.9 | 560 | Glentivar |
| 59 | 10,378 | Point 10,378 | Point 10,715 | 0.6 | 301 | Glentivar |
| 60 | 10,368 | Indian BM | Burntop | 8.9 | 1,038 | Eagle Rock |
|  | 10,363 | Basin2 BM | Reinecker Ridge | 2.5 | 113 | Fairplay East |
| 61 | 10,341 | Point 10,341 | Reinecker Ridge | 3.1 | 355 | Fairplay East |
| 62 | 10,340 | Point 10,340 | Stoll Mtn | 1.6 | 440 | Elevenmile Canyon |
| S | 10,300 | Point 10,300 | Puma Pk | 1.3 | 280 | Farnum Pk |
| 63 | 10,289 | Point 10,289 | Indian BM | 1.2 | 399 | Eagle Rock |
| 64 | 10,274 | Point 10,274 | Reinecker Ridge | 1.4 | 344 | Fairplay East |
| 65 | 10,207 | Point 10,207 | Point 10,715 | 0.9 | 347 | Glentivar |
| 66 | 10,190 | Point 10,190 | South Twin Cone Pk | 4.4 | 307 | Observatory Rock |
| 67 | 10,122 | Mexican Ridge | Point 10,274 | 1.4 | 612 | Elkhorn |
| 68 | 10,093 | Point 10,093 | Point 10,378 | 0.5 | 313 | Glentivar |
| 69 | 10,073 | Observatory Rock | Indian BM | 2.7 | 573 | Observatory Rock |
| 70 | 10,069 | Point 10,069 | Point 10,380 | 1.2 | 649 | Glentivar |
| S | 10,060 | Point 10,060 | Roachaburger | 1.3 | 291 | Glentivar |
| 71 | 10,030 | Point 10,030 | Indian BM | 3.0 | 340 | Elkhorn |
| 72 | 9,986 | Point 9,986 | Point 10,030 | 5.9 | 356 | Elkhorn |
| 73 | 9,951 | Sugarloaf Mtn | Point 11,611 | 2.4 | 467 | Farnum Pk |
|  | 9,940 | X Rock | Point 11,762 | 1.1 | 120 | McCurdy Mtn |
| 74 | 9,928 | Point 9,928 | Indian BM | 2.5 | 388 | Observatory Rock |
|  | 9,921 | Elkhorn BM | Point 9,986 | 1.4 | 271 | Elkhorn |
| 75 | 9,900 | Point 9,900 | Point 10,340 | 2.7 | 840 | Elevenmile Canyon |
| 76 | 9,898 | Mania BM | Point 9,986 | 4.2 | 508 | Sulphur Mtn |
| 77 | 9,895 | Point 9,895 | Burntop | 2.3 | 355 | Eagle Rock |
| 78 | 9,870 | Point 9,870 | Observatory Rock | 1.1 | 330 | Observatory Rock |

## RETIREMENT RANGE–SORTED BY ELEVATION *(continued)*

| Rank | Elev. | Summit Name | Parent | Mile | Rise | Quadrangle |
|---|---|---|---|---|---|---|
| 79 | 9,833 | Point 9,833 | Point 9,986 | 2.0 | 303 | Sulphur Mtn |
| | 9,830 | Logan Hill | Point 9,986 | 1.0 | 180 | Elkhorn |
| 80 | 9,752 | Point 9,752 | Point 10,868 | 2.4 | 452 | Glentivar |
| | 9,726 | Clark BM | Mexican Ridge | 1.8 | 106 | Milligan Lakes |
| 81 | 9,710 | Eagle Rock | Point 9,895 | 2.9 | 500 | Eagle Rock |
| 82 | 9,706 | Point 9,706 | Badger Mtn | 1.6 | 326 | Tarryall |
| 83 | 9,691 | Castle, The | Buffalo Pk | 2.5 | 591 | Windy Pk |
| 84 | 9,556 | Bald Hill | Point 9,619 | 4.1 | 466 | Hartsel |
| | 9,544 | Baker Mtn | Point 10,289 | 2.2 | 154 | Eagle Rock |
| | 9,528 | Link Spring Ridge | Point 10,030 | 2.0 | 98 | Elkhorn |
| 85 | 9,524 | Spinney Mtn | Point 10,069 | 4.0 | 814 | Spinney Mtn |
| 86 | 9,500 | Point 9,500 | Buffalo Pk | 1.5 | 400 | Green Mtn |
| 87 | 9,489 | Bradley Pk | Point 10,462 | 2.5 | 495 | McCurdy Mtn |
| S | 9,422 | Point 9,422 | Point 9,900 | 1.0 | 282 | Elevenmile Canyon |
| 88 | 9,380 | Point 9,380 A | Bradley Pk | 1.3 | 320 | McCurdy Mtn |
| 89 | 9,380 | Point 9,380 B | Pulver Mtn | 1.9 | 320 | Tarryall |
| 90 | 9,339 | Sulphur Mtn | Roachaburger | 4.7 | 529 | Sulphur Mtn |
| | 9,310 | Al Hill | Eagle Rock | 1.8 | 177 | Eagle Rock |
| 91 | 9,300 | Point 9,300 | Point 11,328 | 1.4 | 360 | McCurdy Mtn |
| | 9,300 | Mud Hill | Point 9,928 | 1.7 | 80 | Observatory Rock |
| 92 | 9,242 | Point 9,242 | Point 9,300 | 0.7 | 342 | McCurdy Mtn |
| 93 | 9,241 | Point 9,241 | Point 9,900 | 1.6 | 381 | Elevenmile Canyon |
| | 9,236 | Reese BM | Eagle Rock | 2.7 | 56 | Observatory Rock |
| S | 9,220 | Point 9,220 | Point 9,422 | 0.9 | 280 | Elevenmile Canyon |
| | 9,193 | Rob BM | Point 9,870 | 1.6 | 13 | Observatory Rock |
| 94 | 9,192 | Little Scraggy Pk | Green Mtn | 1.5 | 772 | Green Mtn |
| 95 | 9,189 | China Wall | Point 9,752 | 2.6 | 409 | Tarryall |
| 96 | 9,162 | Point 9,162 | Point 9,241 | 1.5 | 422 | Elevenmile Canyon |
| 97 | 9,137 | Point 9,137 | Point 9,162 | 2.3 | 317 | Tarryall |
| 98 | 9,111 | Point 9,111 | China Wall | 1.3 | 331 | McCurdy Mtn |
| 99 | 9,083 | Point 9,083 | Point 9,137 | 4.5 | 783 | Hackett Mtn |
| 100 | 9,036 | Point 9,036 | Point 9,083 | 2.5 | 536 | Hackett Mtn |
| S | 9,033 | Round Mtn | Point 9,706 | 2.4 | 293 | Tarryall |
| S | 9,020 | Point 9,020 | Point 9,900 | 1.9 | 280 | Elevenmile Canyon |
| 101 | 8,980 | Point 8,980 | Point 9,162 | 1.9 | 360 | Elevenmile Canyon |
| 102 | 8,954 | Tappan Mtn | Point 9,036 | 1.7 | 534 | Tarryall |
| 103 | 8,906 | Point 8,906 | Tappan Mtn | 1.0 | 326 | Tarryall |
| 104 | 8,877 | North Sheeprock | Point 10,654 | 3.4 | 977 | Cheesman Lake |
| 105 | 8,812 | Long Scraggy Pk | Little Scraggy Pk | 4.6 | 1,272 | Deckers |
| 106 | 8,783 | Redskin Mtn | Castle, The | 3.4 | 783 | Green Mtn |

## RETIREMENT RANGE–SORTED BY ELEVATION *(continued)*

| Rank | Elev. | Summit Name | Parent | Mile | Rise | Quadrangle |
|------|-------|-------------|--------|------|------|------------|
| 107 | 8,740 | South Sheeprock | North Sheeprock | 1.7 | 520 | Cheesman Lake |
| 108 | 8,729 | Point 8,729 | Point 9,162 | 1.1 | 309 | Elevenmile Canyon |
| 109 | 8,722 | Point 8,722 | Redskin Mtn | 3.2 | 734 | Bailey |
| 110 | 8,685 | Point 8,685 | Point 9,500 | 2.0 | 465 | Cheesman Lake |
| 111 | 8,671 | East Sheeprock | South Sheeprock | 0.7 | 451 | Cheesman Lake |
| 112 | 8,660 | Point 8,660 | Redskin Mtn | 1.7 | 440 | Windy Pk |
| 113 | 8,659 | Point 8,659 | Point 8,722 | 1.4 | 479 | Windy Pk |
| 114 | 8,501 | Sugarloaf Pk | Point 8,685 | 0.9 | 561 | Cheesman Lake |
| 115 | 8,494 | Point 8,494 | Castle, The | 1.1 | 474 | Green Mtn |
| 116 | 8,484 | Point 8,484 | Point 8,660 | 0.6 | 344 | Green Mtn |
| S | 8,260 | Point 8,260 | Point 8,659 | 0.8 | 280 | Bailey |
| S | 8,232 | Point 8,232 | Sugarloaf Pk | 0.4 | 292 | Green Mtn |
|   | 8,220 | Insmont Hill | Bailey, Mt | 2.0 | 200 | Bailey |
| S | 8,220 | Point 8,220 | Point 8,285 | 0.5 | 280 | Cheesman Lake |
| 117 | 8,183 | Raleigh Pk | Cathedral Spires | 2.9 | 643 | Platte Canyon |
| 118 | 8,140 | Point 8,140 | Redskin Mtn | 2.7 | 400 | Pine |
| 119 | 8,020 | Chair Rocks | Raleigh Pk | 1.4 | 320 | Platte Canyon |
| 120 | 7,980 | Point 7,980 | Point 8,140 | 1.4 | 440 | Pine |
| 121 | 7,933 | Cheesman Mtn | Sugarloaf Pk | 1.2 | 753 | Cheesman Lake |
| 122 | 7,872 | Baldy Pk | Point 8,140 | 1.3 | 332 | Green Mtn |
|   | 7,822 | Wigwam BM | Point 8,685 | 1.9 | 2 | Cheesman Lake |
|   | 7,180 | Skull Rock | Cheesman Mtn | 2.8 | 240 | Deckers |
|   | 6,460 | Eagle Rock | Bennett Mtn | 2.2 | 120 | Platte Canyon |

## RETIREMENT RANGE–SORTED BY SUMMIT NAME

| Rank | Elev. | Summit Name | Parent | Mile | Rise | Quadrangle |
|------|-------|-------------|--------|------|------|------------|
|   | 9,310 | Al Hill | Eagle Rock | 1.8 | 177 | Eagle Rock |
| 31 | 11,294 | Badger Mtn | Schoolmarm Mtn | 6.3 | 1,594 | Glentivar |
|   | 9,544 | Baker Mtn | Point 10,289 | 2.2 | 154 | Eagle Rock |
| 84 | 9,556 | Bald Hill | Point 9,619 | 4.1 | 466 | Hartsel |
| 122 | 7,872 | Baldy Pk | Point 8,140 | 1.3 | 332 | Green Mtn |
|   | 10,363 | Basin2 BM | Reinecker Ridge | 2.5 | 113 | Fairplay East |
| 1 | 12,431 | Bison Pk | Logan, Mt | 19.2 | 2,451 | McCurdy Mtn |
|   | 12,303 | Blaine, Mt | South Twin Cone Pk | 1.0 | 203 | Mt Logan |
| 87 | 9,489 | Bradley Pk | Point 10,462 | 2.5 | 495 | McCurdy Mtn |
| 20 | 11,589 | Buffalo Pk | Windy Pk | 4.2 | 929 | Green Mtn |
| 39 | 11,085 | Burntop | Little Puma | 1.8 | 505 | Farnum Pk |
| 83 | 9,691 | Castle, The | Buffalo Pk | 2.5 | 591 | Windy Pk |
| 119 | 8,020 | Chair Rocks | Raleigh Pk | 1.4 | 320 | Platte Canyon |
| 121 | 7,933 | Cheesman Mtn | Sugarloaf Pk | 1.2 | 753 | Cheesman Lake |

## Retirement Range–Sorted by Summit Name *(continued)*

| Rank | Elev. | Summit Name | Parent | Mile | Rise | Quadrangle |
|------|-------|-------------|--------|------|------|------------|
| 95 | 9,189 | China Wall | Point 9,752 | 2.6 | 409 | Tarryall |
| | 9,726 | Clark BM | Mexican Ridge | 1.8 | 106 | Milligan Lakes |
| 81 | 9,710 | Eagle Rock | Point 9,895 | 2.9 | 500 | Eagle Rock |
| | 6,460 | Eagle Rock | Bennett Mtn | 2.2 | 120 | Platte Canyon |
| 111 | 8,671 | East Sheeprock | South Sheeprock | 0.7 | 451 | Cheesman Lake |
| | 9,921 | Elkhorn BM | Point 9,986 | 1.4 | 271 | Elkhorn |
| | 11,377 | Farnum Pk | Little Puma | 0.6 | 277 | Farnum Pk |
| | 11,871 | Foster BM | South Twin Cone Pk | 1.4 | 211 | Mt Logan |
| 56 | 10,421 | Green Mtn | Buffalo Pk | 4.2 | 1,859 | Green Mtn |
| 60 | 10,368 | Indian BM | Burntop | 8.9 | 1,038 | Eagle Rock |
| | 8,220 | Insmont Hill | Bailey, Mt | 2.0 | 200 | Bailey |
| 8 | 12,100 | Kenosha Pk | South Twin Cone Pk | 2.4 | 320 | Mt Logan |
| 26 | 11,403 | Lake Park Pk | Tarryall Pk | 1.0 | 503 | McCurdy Mtn |
| | 9,528 | Link Spring Ridge | Point 10,030 | 2.0 | 98 | Elkhorn |
| 24 | 11,449 | Little Puma | Puma Pk | 1.1 | 495 | Farnum Pk |
| 94 | 9,192 | Little Scraggy Pk | Green Mtn | 1.5 | 772 | Green Mtn |
| | 9,830 | Logan Hill | Point 9,986 | 1.0 | 180 | Elkhorn |
| 105 | 8,812 | Long Scraggy Pk | Little Scraggy Pk | 4.6 | 1,272 | Deckers |
| 48 | 10,657 | Lost Platte Peak | Point 11,271 | 3.1 | 767 | Windy Pk |
| 76 | 9,898 | Mania BM | Point 9,986 | 4.2 | 508 | Sulphur Mtn |
| 32 | 11,289 | Martland Pk | Schoolmarm Mtn | 1.5 | 463 | Glentivar |
| 7 | 12,168 | McCurdy Mtn | Bison Pk | 2.1 | 789 | McCurdy Mtn |
| 67 | 10,122 | Mexican Ridge | Point 10,274 | 1.4 | 612 | Elkhorn |
| | 9,300 | Mud Hill | Point 9,928 | 1.7 | 80 | Observatory Rock |
| 14 | 11,789 | No Payne | Shawnee Pk | 1.9 | 369 | Shawnee |
| 104 | 8,877 | North Sheeprock | Point 10,654 | 3.4 | 977 | Cheesman Lake |
| 13 | 11,902 | North Tarryall Pk | Pk Z | 3.4 | 872 | Topaz Mtn |
| 4 | 12,323 | North Twin Cone Pk | South Twin Cone Pk | 1.4 | 383 | Mt Logan |
| 69 | 10,073 | Observatory Rock | Indian BM | 2.7 | 573 | Observatory Rock |
| 15 | 11,780 | Payne BM | No Payne | 1.5 | 520 | Topaz Mtn |
| S | 10,624 | Pilot Pk | Point 10,982 | 1.2 | 284 | Tarryall |
| 2 | 12,429 | Pk X | Logan, Mt | 9.0 | 1,749 | Topaz Mtn |
| 5 | 12,274 | Pk Y | Pk X | 1.0 | 534 | Topaz Mtn |
| 6 | 12,244 | Pk Z | Pk Y | 0.7 | 304 | Topaz Mtn |
| 11 | 11,941 | Platte Pk | Kenosha Pk | 1.3 | 401 | Shawnee |
| 17 | 11,762 | Point 11,762 | McCurdy Mtn | 1.1 | 342 | McCurdy Mtn |
| 19 | 11,611 | Point 11,611 | Topaz Mtn | 2.6 | 391 | Topaz Mtn |
| 22 | 11,469 | Point 11,469 | Point 11,611 | 1.6 | 329 | Farnum Pk |
| 23 | 11,460 | Point 11,460 | Point 11,762 | 1.0 | 560 | McCurdy Mtn |
| 25 | 11,423 | Point 11,423 | Point 11,469 | 1.8 | 603 | Topaz Mtn |

125

## RETIREMENT RANGE–SORTED BY SUMMIT NAME *(continued)*

| Rank | Elev. | Summit Name | Parent | Mile | Rise | Quadrangle |
|------|-------|-------------|--------|------|------|------------|
| 27 | 11,391 | Point 11,391 | North Tarryall Pk | 1.5 | 371 | Topaz Mtn |
| 29 | 11,328 | Point 11,328 | Point 11,460 | 0.9 | 468 | McCurdy Mtn |
| 30 | 11,306 | Point 11,306 | Point 11,611 | 1.3 | 326 | Topaz Mtn |
| 33 | 11,271 | Point 11,271 | Windy Pk | 3.4 | 484 | Windy Pk |
| 34 | 11,270 | Point 11,270 | Point 11,391 | 1.4 | 370 | Topaz Mtn |
| 35 | 11,230 | Point 11,230 | Windy Pk | 2.7 | 1,090 | Windy Pk |
| 37 | 11,180 | Point 11,180 A | Point 11,230 | 1.3 | 400 | Windy Pk |
| 38 | 11,180 | Point 11,180 B | McCurdy Mtn | 1.2 | 360 | McCurdy Mtn |
| 40 | 11,060 | Point 11,060 | Point 11,271 | 2.1 | 579 | Topaz Mtn |
| 41 | 11,053 | Point 11,053 | Badger Mtn | 0.8 | 313 | Glentivar |
| 42 | 10,982 | Point 10,982 | South Tarryall Pk | 2.5 | 482 | McCurdy Mtn |
| 43 | 10,926 | Point 10,926 | Point 11,230 | 0.6 | 306 | Windy Pk |
| 45 | 10,868 | Point 10,868 | Martland Pk | 2.3 | 848 | Farnum Pk |
| 46 | 10,721 | Point 10,721 | Schoolmarm Mtn | 1.4 | 341 | Farnum Pk |
| 47 | 10,715 | Point 10,715 | Martland Pk | 0.8 | 453 | Glentivar |
| 49 | 10,654 | Point 10,654 | Point 11,180 A | 2.9 | 634 | McCurdy Mtn |
| S | 10,624 | Point 10,624 | Point 11,391 | 1.6 | 284 | Observatory Rock |
| 50 | 10,620 | Point 10,620 | Point 11,180 A | 1.0 | 560 | Windy Pk |
| 51 | 10,605 | Point 10,605 | Point 10,654 | 1.2 | 305 | McCurdy Mtn |
| 52 | 10,568 | Point 10,568 | Point 11,053 | 1.2 | 308 | Glentivar |
| 55 | 10,462 | Point 10,462 | Point 10,868 | 1.6 | 678 | Farnum Pk |
| 58 | 10,380 | Point 10,380 | Pulver Mtn | 0.9 | 560 | Glentivar |
| 59 | 10,378 | Point 10,378 | Point 10,715 | 0.6 | 301 | Glentivar |
| 61 | 10,341 | Point 10,341 | Reinecker Ridge | 3.1 | 355 | Fairplay East |
| 62 | 10,340 | Point 10,340 | Stoll Mtn | 1.6 | 440 | Elevenmile Canyon |
| S | 10,300 | Point 10,300 | Puma Pk | 1.3 | 280 | Farnum Pk |
| 63 | 10,289 | Point 10,289 | Indian BM | 1.2 | 399 | Eagle Rock |
| 64 | 10,274 | Point 10,274 | Reinecker Ridge | 1.4 | 344 | Fairplay East |
| 65 | 10,207 | Point 10,207 | Point 10,715 | 0.9 | 347 | Glentivar |
| 66 | 10,190 | Point 10,190 | South Twin Cone Pk | 4.4 | 307 | Observatory Rock |
| 68 | 10,093 | Point 10,093 | Point 10,378 | 0.5 | 313 | Glentivar |
| 70 | 10,069 | Point 10,069 | Point 10,380 | 1.2 | 649 | Glentivar |
| S | 10,060 | Point 10,060 | Roachaburger | 1.3 | 291 | Glentivar |
| 71 | 10,030 | Point 10,030 | Indian BM | 3.0 | 340 | Elkhorn |
| 72 | 9,986 | Point 9,986 | Point 10,030 | 5.9 | 356 | Elkhorn |
| 74 | 9,928 | Point 9,928 | Indian BM | 2.5 | 388 | Observatory Rock |
| 75 | 9,900 | Point 9,900 | Point 10,340 | 2.7 | 840 | Elevenmile Canyon |
| 77 | 9,895 | Point 9,895 | Burntop | 2.3 | 355 | Eagle Rock |
| 78 | 9,870 | Point 9,870 | Observatory Rock | 1.1 | 330 | Observatory Rock |
| 79 | 9,833 | Point 9,833 | Point 9,986 | 2.0 | 303 | Sulphur Mtn |

## RETIREMENT RANGE–SORTED BY SUMMIT NAME *(continued)*

| Rank | Elev. | Summit Name | Parent | Mile | Rise | Quadrangle |
|------|-------|-------------|--------|------|------|------------|
| 80 | 9,752 | Point 9,752 | Point 10,868 | 2.4 | 452 | Glentivar |
| 82 | 9,706 | Point 9,706 | Badger Mtn | 1.6 | 326 | Tarryall |
| 86 | 9,500 | Point 9,500 | Buffalo Pk | 1.5 | 400 | Green Mtn |
| S | 9,422 | Point 9,422 | Point 9,900 | 1.0 | 282 | Elevenmile Canyon |
| 88 | 9,380 | Point 9,380 A | Bradley Pk | 1.3 | 320 | McCurdy Mtn |
| 89 | 9,380 | Point 9,380 B | Pulver Mtn | 1.9 | 320 | Tarryall |
| 91 | 9,300 | Point 9,300 | Point 11,328 | 1.4 | 360 | McCurdy Mtn |
| 92 | 9,242 | Point 9,242 | Point 9,300 | 0.7 | 342 | McCurdy Mtn |
| 93 | 9,241 | Point 9,241 | Point 9,900 | 1.6 | 381 | Elevenmile Canyon |
| S | 9,220 | Point 9,220 | Point 9,422 | 0.9 | 280 | Elevenmile Canyon |
| 96 | 9,162 | Point 9,162 | Point 9,241 | 1.5 | 422 | Elevenmile Canyon |
| 97 | 9,137 | Point 9,137 | Point 9,162 | 2.3 | 317 | Tarryall |
| 98 | 9,111 | Point 9,111 | China Wall | 1.3 | 331 | McCurdy Mtn |
| 99 | 9,083 | Point 9,083 | Point 9,137 | 4.5 | 783 | Hackett Mtn |
| 100 | 9,036 | Point 9,036 | Point 9,083 | 2.5 | 536 | Hackett Mtn |
| S | 9,020 | Point 9,020 | Point 9,900 | 1.9 | 280 | Elevenmile Canyon |
| 101 | 8,980 | Point 8,980 | Point 9,162 | 1.9 | 360 | Elevenmile Canyon |
| 103 | 8,906 | Point 8,906 | Tappan Mtn | 1.0 | 326 | Tarryall |
| 108 | 8,729 | Point 8,729 | Point 9,162 | 1.1 | 309 | Elevenmile Canyon |
| 109 | 8,722 | Point 8,722 | Redskin Mtn | 3.2 | 734 | Bailey |
| 110 | 8,685 | Point 8,685 | Point 9,500 | 2.0 | 465 | Cheesman Lake |
| 112 | 8,660 | Point 8,660 | Redskin Mtn | 1.7 | 440 | Windy Pk |
| 113 | 8,659 | Point 8,659 | Point 8,722 | 1.4 | 479 | Windy Pk |
| 115 | 8,494 | Point 8,494 | Castle, The | 1.1 | 474 | Green Mtn |
| 116 | 8,484 | Point 8,484 | Point 8,660 | 0.6 | 344 | Green Mtn |
| S | 8,260 | Point 8,260 | Point 8,659 | 0.8 | 280 | Bailey |
| S | 8,232 | Point 8,232 | Sugarloaf Pk | 0.4 | 292 | Green Mtn |
| S | 8,220 | Point 8,220 | Point 8,285 | 0.5 | 280 | Cheesman Lake |
| 118 | 8,140 | Point 8,140 | Redskin Mtn | 2.7 | 400 | Pine |
| 120 | 7,980 | Point 7,980 | Point 8,140 | 1.4 | 440 | Pine |
| 54 | 10,538 | Pulver Mtn | Stoll Mtn | 1.6 | 318 | Glentivar |
| 21 | 11,570 | Puma Pk | Point 11,762 | 7.3 | 2,240 | Farnum Pk |
| 117 | 8,183 | Raleigh Pk | Cathedral Spires | 2.9 | 643 | Platte Canyon |
| 106 | 8,783 | Redskin Mtn | Castle, The | 3.4 | 783 | Green Mtn |
| | 9,236 | Reese BM | Eagle Rock | 2.7 | 56 | Observatory Rock |
| 53 | 10,558 | Reinecker Ridge | Little Baldy Mtn | 7.8 | 811 | Fairplay East |
| | 10,460 | Rishaberger Mtn | Schoolmarm Mtn | 1.3 | 240 | Glentivar |
| 57 | 10,412 | Roachaburger | Schoolmarm Mtn | 2.0 | 392 | Sulphur Mtn |
| | 9,193 | Rob BM | Point 9,870 | 1.6 | 13 | Observatory Rock |
| S | 9,033 | Round Mtn | Point 9,706 | 2.4 | 293 | Tarryall |

## RETIREMENT RANGE–SORTED BY SUMMIT NAME *(continued)*

| Rank | Elev. | Summit Name | Parent | Mile | Rise | Quadrangle |
|------|-------|-------------|--------|------|------|------------|
| 28 | 11,332 | Schoolmarm Mtn | Puma Pk | 2.7 | 632 | Glentivar |
| 12 | 11,927 | Shawnee Pk | Platte Pk | 1.3 | 307 | Shawnee |
| | 7,180 | Skull Rock | Cheesman Mtn | 2.8 | 240 | Deckers |
| 107 | 8,740 | South Sheeprock | North Sheeprock | 1.7 | 520 | Cheesman Lake |
| 36 | 11,206 | South Tarryall Pk | Point 11,403 | 1.7 | 1,186 | McCurdy Mtn |
| 3 | 12,340 | South Twin Cone Pk | Pk X | 5.2 | 720 | Mt Logan |
| 85 | 9,524 | Spinney Mtn | Point 10,069 | 4.0 | 814 | Spinney Mtn |
| 44 | 10,879 | Stoll Mtn | Badger Pk | 4.0 | 1,379 | Spinney Mtn |
| 73 | 9,951 | Sugarloaf Mtn | Point 11,611 | 2.4 | 467 | Farnum Pk |
| 114 | 8,501 | Sugarloaf Pk | Point 8,685 | 0.9 | 561 | Cheesman Lake |
| 90 | 9,339 | Sulphur Mtn | Roachaburger | 4.7 | 529 | Sulphur Mtn |
| 102 | 8,954 | Tappan Mtn | Point 9,036 | 1.7 | 534 | Tarryall |
| 16 | 11,780 | Tarryall Pk | McCurdy Mtn | 2.7 | 920 | McCurdy Mtn |
| 18 | 11,762 | Topaz Mtn | North Tarryall Pk | 2.4 | 662 | Topaz Mtn |
| | 7,822 | Wigwam BM | Point 8,685 | 1.9 | 2 | Cheesman Lake |
| 10 | 11,970 | Windy Pk | Bison Pk | 5.4 | 1,510 | Windy Pk |
| S | 12,100 | X Prime | Pk X | 0.7 | 280 | Topaz Mtn |
| | 9,940 | X Rock | Point 11,762 | 1.1 | 120 | McCurdy Mtn |
| 9 | 12,067 | Zephyr | Pk Z | 1.0 | 337 | Topaz Mtn |

# INDEX

**Note:** italic page numbers indicate photographs and maps.

140

# ABOUT THE AUTHORS

Gerry Roach is a world-class mountaineer. After climbing Mount Everest in 1983, he went on to become the second person to climb the highest peak on each of the seven continents in 1985. In 6 decades of mountaineering, Gerry has climbed in dozens of states and countries. He has been on 15 Alaskan expeditions, 10 Andean expeditions and 7 Himalayan expeditions, including first ascents in the kingdom of Bhutan. In 1997, he summited Gasherbrum II in the Karakorum. In 2000, he became the first person to climb North America's 10 highest peaks. He is a member of the American Alpine Club.

Closer to home, Gerry has climbed more than 1,200 named peaks in Colorado, including all the fourteeners, which he completed for the first time in 1975. He finished climbing every named peak in the Indian Peaks Wilderness and Rocky Mountain National Park in 1978. He has also climbed every peak in the Colorado counties of Boulder, Gilpin and Clear Creek, and every named peak in Jefferson County.

Gerry is also an accomplished rock climber. His first book, *Flatiron Classics,* is a guide to the trails and easier rock climbs in the Flatirons above Boulder. His second book, *Rocky Mountain National Park,* is a guide to the classic hikes and climbs in that park. Gerry's guide *Colorado's Indian Peaks,* now in its second edition, remains the definitive mountaineering guide to that special area. In his guide *Colorado's Fourteeners,* he shares his intimate knowledge of and love for Colorado's high peaks. With this book on the Lost Creek Wilderness, Gerry expands the scope of his guidebooks and continues to convey his love for Colorado's mountains. He climbed his first Colorado peak in 1956 and continues to climb actively today, returning to Colorado's mountains to hone his skills. Mountaineering in this rugged and beautiful state forms the foundation for his successful expeditions to the Earth's great peaks.

Jennifer Roach is an expert on Colorado's mountains. She has climbed Colorado's 500 highest peaks and is close to finishing all of the state's thirteeners. She has climbed Colorado's mountains for 20 years and knows all about places most of us have never heard of. Jennifer has visited the Lost Creek Wilderness for most of these years and has led many Colorado Mountain Club trips there. She has summited most of the peaks in the Lost Creek Wilderness more than once. She introduced Gerry to this area and climbed all the peaks again with him.

Gerry and Jennifer live in Boulder, Colorado.